EXPERIENCING
the WORDS *of*
Jesus

EXPERIENCING

the WORDS *of*

Jesus

HEARING HIS VOICE

TRUSTING HIS WORDS

MAX LUCADO

THOMAS NELSON
Since 1798

NASHVILLE   DALLAS   MEXICO CITY   RIO DE JANEIRO   BEIJING

EXPERIENCING *the* WORDS *of* Jesus

© 2008 Max Lucado.

Published in Nashville, Tennessee, by Thomas Nelson. Thomas Nelson is a registered trademark of Thomas Nelson, Inc.

Thomas Nelson, Inc., titles may be purchased in bulk for educational, business, fund-raising, or sales promotional use. For information, please e-mail SpecialMarkets@ThomasNelson.com.

978-0-8499-2127-8

Printed in the United States of America
08 09 10 11 QW 9 8 7 6 5 4 3 2 1

CONTENTS

The Simple Sentence

Here's a toast to the simple sentence.

Here's a salute to one-liners.

Join me in applauding the delete key and the eraser. May they feast on the trimmings of the writer's table.

I believe in brevity. Cut the fat and keep the fact. Give us words to chew on, not words to wade through. Thoughts that spark, not lines that drag. More periods. Fewer commas.

Distill it.

Barebone it.

Bareknuckle it.

Concise (but not cute). Clear (but not shallow). Vivid (but not detailed). That's good writing. That's good reading. But that's hard work!

But, it's what we like. We appreciate the chef who cuts the gristle before he serves the steak. We salute the communicator who does the same.

Ahhh, brevity. An art apparently unheeded in the realms of insurance brochures and some-assembly-required bicycle manuals.

We learn brevity from Jesus. His greatest sermon can be read in eight minutes (Matthew 5–7). His best-known story can be read in ninety seconds (Luke 15:11–32). He summarized prayer in five phrases (Matthew 6:9–13). He silenced accusers with one challenge (John 8:7). He rescued a soul with one sentence (Luke 23:43). He summarized the

Jesus' ministry on this earth lasted only three and a half years, yet in that time his words turned heads, turned hearts, and ultimately turned the world upside down.

Law in three verses (Mark 12:29–31), and he reduced all his teachings to one command (John 15:12).

He made his point and went home.

Jesus' ministry on this earth lasted only three and a half years, yet in that time his words turned heads, turned hearts, and ultimately turned the world upside down. The words of Jesus offer much to those who have ears to hear. They are his legacy. They are our heritage.

In this workbook you will have the opportunity to hear his voice for yourself. Words made indistinct by the hubbub of daily life will ring in your ears with renewed clarity. Let his still, small voice echo through your heart.

There are a total of six lessons—each divided into daily sections. Begin with prayer, asking the Lord for wisdom, insight, and determination. Read the stories; hear his voice. There are questions to send you into the rest of the Scriptures—teaching your heart to recognize his words, his truth. The one who speaks also listens, so there is also ample space to journal. Share with the Lord your thoughts, feelings, and hopes.

The words of Christ—discourses, parables, prayers, conversations. Eminently quotable. Undeniably powerful. Eternally true. Let the message that changed the world change your life forever.

Selection taken from *When God Whispers Your Name*

LESSON ONE

He's Calling

THERE ARE TIMES when we see. And there are times when we *see*. Let me show you what I mean:

Everything changes the morning you see the "for sale" sign on your neighbor's boat. His deluxe bass boat. The bass boat you've coveted for three summers. All of a sudden nothing else matters. A gravitational tug pulls your car to the curb. You sigh as you behold your dream glistening in the sun. You run your fingers along the edge, pausing only to wipe the drool from your shirt. As you gaze, you are transported to Lake Tamapwantee, and it's just you and the glassy waters and your bass boat.

Or perhaps the following paragraph describes you better:

Everything changes the day you see him enter the English lit classroom. Just enough swagger to be cool. Just enough smarts to be classy. Not walking so fast as to be nervous, nor so slow as to be cocky. You've seen him before, but only in your dreams. Now he's really here. And you can't take

They followed Jesus. Then Jesus turned, and seeing them following, said to them, "What do you seek?" They said to Him, "Rabbi" (which is to say, when translated, Teacher), "where are You staying?" He said to them, "Come and see."
JOHN 1:37–39

your eyes off him. By the time class is over, you've memorized every curl and lash. And by the time this day is over, you resolve he's going to be yours.

There are times when we see. And then there are times when we *see*. There are times when we observe, and there are times when we memorize. There are times when we notice, and there are times when we study. Most of us know what it means to see a new boat or a new boy . . . but do we know what it's like to see Jesus?

1. In Acts 26:12–18, Paul recounts his experience on the road to Damascus when he saw the Lord. At the very moment his eyes were blinded, they were opened. What did Jesus ask of Paul that day, according to verses 17–18?

_____

_____

_____

> But without faith it is impossible to please Him, for he who comes to God must believe that He is, and that He is a rewarder of those who diligently seek Him.
>
> HEBREWS 11:6

2. You won't see Jesus if you're not looking for him. What does Hebrews 11:6 say that God rewards?

_____

_____

3. God has been beckoning to us since the beginning, calling for people to see his hand, to hear his voice, and to seek his face.

   • 1 Chronicles 22:19—What did David command the people to do when building the temple?

   _____

   _____

- Isaiah 55:6—According to Isaiah, when should we seek the Lord? When should we call out to him?

_____

_____

_____

- Hosea 10:12—According to Hosea, what are we to plant? What will we reap? If we seek the Lord, what will we see him do?

_____

_____

_____

Consider John and Andrew. They were rewarded for seeking out Jesus. For them it wasn't enough to listen to John the Baptist. Most would have been content to serve in the shadow of the world's most famous evangelist. Could there be a better teacher? Only one. And when John and Andrew saw him, they left John the Baptist and followed Jesus. Note the request they made.

"Rabbi," they asked, "where are you staying?" (John 1:38 NIV). Pretty bold request. They didn't ask Jesus to give them a minute or an opinion or a message or a miracle. They asked for his address. They wanted to hang out with him. They wanted to know him. They wanted to know what caused his head to turn and his heart to burn and his soul to yearn. They wanted to study his eyes and follow his steps. They wanted to see him.

Jesus' answer to the disciples? "Come and see." He didn't say, "Come and glance," or "Come and peek." He said, "Come and see." Bring your bifocals and binoculars. This is no time for side-glances or occasional peeks. "Let us fix our eyes on Jesus, the author and perfecter of our faith" (Hebrews 12:2 NIV).

The fisherman fixes his eyes on the boat. The girl fixes her eyes on the boy. The disciple fixes his eyes on the Savior.

4. God makes a promise to those who seek him. In fact, we find the same promise repeated time and again in the Bible.

- How does God want to be sought, according to Deuteronomy 4:29?

_____

_____

_____

- When will we find the Lord, according to the prophet in Jeremiah 29:13?

_____

_____

_____

- What does Jesus reveal in Matthew 7:7?

_____

_____

_____

When You said, "Seek My face," my heart said to You, "Your face, LORD, I will seek."

PSALM 27:8

5. What do we learn about seekers in Lamentations 3:25?

_____

_____

_____

Zacchaeus was far from a big guy. He was small, so small he couldn't see over the crowd that lined the street the day Jesus came to Jericho. Of course the crowd might have let him elbow up to the front, except that he was a tax collector. But he had a hunger in his heart to see Jesus.

It wasn't enough to stand at the back of the crowd. It wasn't enough to peer through a cardboard telescope. It wasn't enough to listen to someone else describe the parade of the Messiah. Zacchaeus wanted to see Jesus with his own eyes.

So he went out on a limb. Clad in a three-piece Armani suit and brand-new Italian loafers, he shimmied up a tree in hopes of seeing Christ.

6. Zacchaeus was in earnest. He was willing to go out on a limb in his search for something to trust. What assurance can we draw from Psalm 9:10?

_____

_____

_____

_____

7. Those who seek the Lord are rewarded for their diligence. Take a look at these scriptures, and match each verse with the additional rewards we receive when we find him.

____ Psalm 27:4   a. We shall be "happy" or "blessed."

____ Psalm 34:4   b. We will dwell with him, seeing his beauty firsthand.

____ Psalm 105:4   c. God listens to us.

____ Psalm 119:2   d. He delivers us from our fears.

____ Ephesians 2:18   e. He lends us his strength.

Would you go out on a limb to see Jesus? Not everyone would. In the same Bible where we read about Zacchaeus crawling across the limb, we read about a young ruler. Unlike the way they treated Zacchaeus, the crowd parted to make room for him. He was the . . . ahem . . . *rich, young ruler.* Upon learning that Jesus was in the area, he called for the limo and cruised across town and approached the carpenter. Please note the question he had for Jesus: "Teacher, what good thing must I do to have life forever?" (Matthew 19:16 NCV).

Bottom line sort of fellow, this ruler. No time for formalities or conversations. "Let's get right to the issue. Your schedule is busy; so is mine. Tell me how I can get saved, and I'll leave you alone."

There was nothing wrong with his question, but there was a problem with his heart. Contrast his desire with that of Zacchaeus: "Can I make it up that tree?"

Or John and Andrew: "Where are you staying?" (John 1:38 NIV).

Or Matthew: "Can you spend the evening?"

See the difference? The rich, young ruler wanted medicine. The others wanted the Physician. The ruler wanted an answer to the quiz. They wanted the teacher. He was in a hurry. They had all the time in the world. He settled for a cup of coffee at the drive-through window. They wouldn't settle for anything less than a full-course meal at the banquet table. They wanted more than salvation. They wanted the Savior. They wanted to see Jesus.

8. How does Psalm 69:32 characterize those who seek God?

_____

_____

_____

9. Scripture tells us how to go about our search. In fact, Peter and Paul offer the same advice.

- 2 Peter 3:14

_____

_____

_____

_____

- 2 Timothy 2:15

_____

_____

_____

_____

Diligently—what a great word. Be diligent in your search. Be hungry in your quest, relentless in your pilgrimage. Step away from the puny pursuits of possessions and positions, and seek your king. Do as John and Andrew did: ask for his address. Do as Matthew: invite Jesus into your house. Imitate Zacchaeus. Risk whatever it takes to see Christ. ✵

DAY TWO
I will make you fishers of men . . .

Then Jesus said to them, "Follow Me, and I will make you become fishers of men."
MARK 1:17

WHEN I WAS in high school, our family used to fish every year during spring break. One year my brother and my mom couldn't go, so my dad let me invite a friend. I asked Mark. He was a good pal and a great sport. He got permission from his parents, and we began planning our trip.

Days before leaving, we could already anticipate the vacation. We could feel the sun warming our bodies as we floated in the boat. We could feel the yank of the rod and hear the spin of the reel as we wrestled the white bass into the boat. And we could smell the fish frying in an open skillet over an open fire.

We could hardly wait. Days passed like cold molasses. Finally spring break arrived. We loaded our camper and set out for the lake.

We arrived late at night, unfolded the camper, and went to bed—dreaming of tomorrow's day in the sun. But during the night, an unseasonably strong norther blew in. It got cold fast! The wind was so strong that we could barely open the camper door the next morning. The sky was gray. The lake was a mountain range of white-topped waves. There was no way we could fish in that weather.

"No problem," we said. "We'll spend the day in the camper. After all, we have Monopoly. We have *Reader's Digest.* We all know a few jokes. It's not what we came to do, but we'll make the best of it and fish tomorrow."

So, huddled in the camper with a Coleman stove and a Monopoly board, we three fishermen passed the day—

indoors. The hours passed slowly, but they did pass. Night finally came, and we crawled into the sleeping bags, dreaming of angling.

Were we in for a surprise. The next morning it wasn't the wind that made the door hard to open; it was the ice!

We tried to be cheerful. "No problem," we mumbled. "We can play Monopoly . . . again. We can reread the stories in *Reader's Digest.* And surely we know another joke or two." But as courageous as we tried to be, it was obvious that some of the gray had left the sky and entered our camper.

I began to notice a few things I hadn't seen before. I noticed that Mark had a few personality flaws. He was a bit too cocky about his opinions. He was easily irritated and constantly edgy. He couldn't take any constructive criticism. Even though his socks did stink, he didn't think it was my business to tell him.

"Just looking out for the best interest of my dad's camper," I defended, expecting Dad to come to my aid.

But Dad just sat over in the corner, reading. *Humph,* I thought, *where is he when I need him?* And then, I began to see Dad in a different light. When I mentioned to him that the eggs were soggy and the toast was burnt, he invited me to try my hand at the portable stove. *Touchy, touchy,* I said to myself. *Nothing like being cooped up in a camper with someone to help you see his real nature.*

It was a long day. It was a long, cold night.

When we awoke the next morning to the sound of sleet slapping the canvas, we didn't even pretend to be cheerful. We were flat-out grumpy. Mark became more of a jerk with each passing moment; I wondered what spell of ignorance I must have been in when I invited him. Dad couldn't do anything right; I wondered how someone so irritable could have such an even-tempered son. We sat in misery the whole day, our fishing equipment still unpacked.

The next day was even colder. "We're going home" were my father's first words. No one objected.

I learned a hard lesson that week. Not about fishing, but about people.

When those who are called to fish don't fish, they fight.

When energy intended to be used outside is used inside, the result is explosive. Instead of casting nets, we cast stones. Instead of extending helping hands, we point accusing fingers. Instead of being fishers of the lost, we become critics of the saved. Rather than helping the hurting, we hurt the helpers.

1. What was Jesus' plan for his followers from the moment he called them, according to Mark 1:17?

_____

_____

_____

God . . . has saved us and called us with a holy calling, not according to our works, but according to His own purpose and grace which was given to us in Christ Jesus before time began.

2 TIMOTHY 1:8–9

2. What do Romans 8:28 and 2 Timothy 1:9 tell us about our own calling?

_____

_____

_____

3. Once the disciples were given this new mission, Jesus showed them the heart of it. What does Matthew 14:14 tell us about the Lord's attitude toward those in need?

_____

_____

_____

The Greek word used for compassion in this passage is *splanchnizomai,* which won't mean much to you unless you are in the health professions and studied splanchnology in school. If so, you remember that splanchnology is a study of the visceral parts. Or, in contemporary jargon, a study of the gut.

When Matthew writes that Jesus had compassion on the people, he is not saying that Jesus felt casual pity for them. No, the term is far more graphic. Matthew is saying that Jesus felt their hurt in his gut:

- He felt the limp of the crippled.
- He felt the hurt of the diseased.
- He felt the loneliness of the leper.
- He felt the embarrassment of the sinful.

And once he felt their hurts, he couldn't help but heal their hurts. He was moved in the stomach by their needs. He was so touched by their needs that he forgot his own needs. He was so moved by the people's hurts that he put his hurts on the back burner.

4. Maybe that's why God brings hurting people into your world too. All solitude and no service equal selfishness. Some solitude and some service, however, equal perspective. What was Jesus' perspective—and prayer request—in Matthew 9:36–38?

_____

_____

_____

5. Compassion is one of God's attributes, tied closely to his mercy and graciousness. Look over the following list, and consider which of these truths you've encountered in your life.

____ God's heart is touched by our struggles, and his mercy is endless (Lamentations 3:19–23).

____ In his compassion, God takes care of his beloved children (Isaiah 58:11).

____ In the aftermath of terrible trials, God's compassion can be seen (James 5:11).

____ God's patience extends even to those who make the same mistakes time and again (Psalm 78:38).

____ The compassion of God made a way for the forgiveness of our sins (Micah 7:19).

____ Jesus' compassion is so great because he knows how we feel (Hebrews 4:14–15).

6. How do we show compassion for one another, according to Galatians 6:2?

_____

_____

_____

When those who are called to fish don't fish, they fight. But note the other side of this fish tale: When those who are called to fish, fish—they flourish!

Nothing handles a case of the gripes like an afternoon service project. Nothing restores perspective better than a visit to a hospital ward. Nothing unites soldiers better than a common task.

7. In Romans 12:15, how does Paul describe the way believers express their compassion for one another?

_____

_____

_____

8. Peter called believers to unity and compassion. How does he describe our attitude and behavior toward one another in 1 Peter 3:8–9?

_____

_____

_____

Again, when those who are called to fish, fish—they flourish! The next time the challenges "outside" tempt you to shut the door and stay inside, stay long enough to get warm. Then get out. When those who are called to fish don't fish, they fight. ✳

Thus says the LORD of hosts: "Execute true justice, show mercy and compassion everyone to his brother."

ZECHARIAH 7:9

DAY THREE
My sheep hear my voice . . .

My sheep hear My voice, and I know them, and they follow Me.
JOHN 10:27

THE MARK OF A SHEEP is its ability to hear the Shepherd's voice.

"The sheep listen to his voice. He calls his own sheep by name and leads them out" (John 10:3 NIV).

The mark of a disciple is his or her ability to hear the Master's voice.

"Here I am! I stand at the door and knock. If anyone hears my voice and opens the door, I will come in and eat with him, and he with me" (Revelation 3:20 NIV).

The world rams at your door; Jesus taps at your door. The voices scream for your allegiance; Jesus softly and tenderly requests it. The world promises flashy pleasure; Jesus promises a quiet dinner . . . with God. "I will come in and eat."

Which voice do you hear?

Let me state something important. There is never a time during which Jesus is not speaking. Never. There is never a place in which Jesus is not present. Never. There is never a room so dark . . . a lounge so sensual . . . an office so sophisticated . . . that the ever-present, ever-pursuing, relentlessly tender Friend is not there, tapping gently on the doors of our hearts—waiting to be invited in.

Few hear his voice. Fewer still open the door.

But never interpret our numbness as his absence. For amidst the fleeting promises of pleasure is the timeless promise of his presence.

1. Comparisons are frequently drawn between people and sheep in the Scriptures.

   • How does Psalm 78:52–53 describe God's care of his people during the Exodus?

   _____

   _____

   • What does the psalmist call people in Psalm 79:13?

   _____

   _____

   • According to Psalm 119:176, what are sheep prone to do?

   _____

   _____

2. God had stern words for the irresponsible "shepherds" of Israel who put their own wants ahead of the good of his people. How does the Lord describe the state of affairs in Ezekiel 34:5–6?

   _____

   _____

   _____

   _____

3. For this reason, God made several promises.

   • What does he say in Ezekiel 34:11 that he plans to do?

   _____

   _____

   _____

- How will the flock be cared for, according to verse 15?

_____

_____

_____

- In verse 23, what does God say will happen?

_____

_____

_____

- What statement, in verse 31, closes this chapter?

_____

_____

_____

4. What comfort do you take from the description in Isaiah 40:11 of God's tender care of those who are his?

_____

_____

_____

_____

5. In the New Testament, Jesus is said to lead his sheep. How does Hebrews 13:20 describe him?

_____

_____

_____

6. The Father's care for his flock was seen in Jesus. How does Jesus refer to himself in John 10:14?

_____

_____

_____

_____

7. Jesus says he is known by his own. How is he known, according to John 10:4–5?

_____

_____

_____

_____

8. All the apostles heard Jesus' voice and knew him—even Paul. In Acts 22:14, Paul shares what Ananias was sent to tell him in the days after his Damascus experience. According to that devout man, what three things was Paul chosen to know and see and hear?

_____

_____

_____

_____

9. What does John 5:28 tell us will occur one day?

_____

_____

_____

_____

Voices that encourage and affirm are distant. But voices that tantalize and entice are near. Voices. Some for pleasure. Some for power. Some promise acceptance. Some promise tenderness. But all promise something.

IN THE EYE OF THE STORM

Interesting. A day is coming when everyone will hear his voice. A day is coming when all the other voices will be silenced; his voice—and his voice only—will be heard.

Some will hear his voice for the very first time. It's not that he never spoke; it's just that they never listened. For these, God's voice will be the voice of a stranger. They will hear it once—and never hear it again. They will spend eternity fending off the voices they followed on earth.

But others will be called from their graves by a familiar voice. For they are sheep who know their shepherd. They are servants who opened the door when Jesus knocked.

Now the door will open again. Only this time, it won't be Jesus who walks into our house; it will be we who walk into his. ✳

IT'S A FACT of the farm. The most fertile ground remains barren if no seed is sown.

Apparently Nicodemus didn't know that. He thought the soil could bear fruit with no seeds. He was big on the farmer's part but forgetful of the seed's part. Nicodemus was a Pharisee, and Pharisees taught that faith was an outside job. What you wore, how you acted, the title you carried, the sound of your prayers, the amount of your gifts—all these were the Pharisees' measure of spirituality.

Had they been farmers, they would have had the most attractive acreage in the region—painted silos and sparkling equipment. The fences would have been whitewashed and clean. The soil overturned and watered.

Had they been farmers, they would have spent hours in the coffee shop discussing the theory of farming. Is it best to fertilize before or after a rain? Do you fallow a field every other year or every third year? Should a farmer wear overalls or jeans? Cowboy hats or baseball caps?

The Pharisees had only one problem. For all their discussion about the right techniques, they harvested little fruit. In fact, one untrained Galilean had borne more fruit in a few short months than all the Pharisees had in a generation. This made them jealous. Angry. Condescending. And they dealt with him by ignoring his results and insulting his methods.

"Rabbi, we know that You are a teacher come from God; for no one can do these signs that You do unless God is with him." Jesus answered and said to him, "Most assuredly, I say to you, unless one is born again, he cannot see the kingdom of God."
JOHN 3:2–3

That is, all the Pharisees except Nicodemus. He was curious. No, more than curious, he was stirred, stirred by the way people listened to Jesus. They listened as if he were the only one with truth. As if he were a prophet.

1. What was important to the Pharisees, according to Matthew 23:1–7?

   _____

   _____

   _____

2. These religious leaders were very concerned with appearances. Why does Jesus call the scribes and Pharisees hypocrites in Matthew 23:25, 27?

   _____

   _____

   _____

3. How does 1 Samuel 16:7 help us understand why God is unimpressed by those who make a good show of righteousness?

   _____

   _____

   _____

When the pressure is on in your life, are you ever tempted to look outside for the problem? Be honest, now. Ever blamed your plight on Washington? (If they'd lower the tax rates, my business would work.) Inculpated your family for your failure? (Mom always liked my sister more.) Called God to account for your problems? (If he is God, why doesn't he heal my marriage?) Faulted the church for your frail faith? (Those people are a bunch of hypocrites.)

Reminds me of the golfer about to hit his first shot on the first hole. He swung and missed the ball. Swung again and whiffed again. Tried a third time and still hit nothing but air. In frustration he looked at his buddies and judged, "Man, this is a tough course."

Now, he may have been right. The course may have been tough. But that wasn't the problem. You may be right, as well. Your circumstances may be challenging, but blaming them is not the solution. Nor is neglecting them.

4. Jesus answered Nicodemus, but his answers caught the Pharisee off guard.

- According to John 3:3, what is required before one can see and be a part of the kingdom of God?

_____

_____

_____

- According to John 3:5–6, how can one be born again?

_____

_____

_____

5. Because of this second birth, what are believers privileged to be called, according to John 1:12–13?

_____

_____

_____

6. Jesus' conversation with Nicodemus isn't the only occasion in the New Testament when this new birth is discussed.

    • What are we born again to, according to 1 Peter 1:3?

    _____

    _____

    • How does 1 Peter 1:23 further describe our new life?

    _____

    _____

    • According to 1 John 2:29, who is born of God?

    _____

Everyone who believes that Jesus is the Christ is born of God, and everyone who loves the father loves his child as well.

—1 JOHN 5:1 NIV

7. This is a soul-deep change that starts on the inside and works its way out. What changes, according to 2 Corinthians 5:17?

    _____

    _____

    _____

8. How does Romans 6:4 describe the possibilities?

    _____

    _____

    _____

9. What does Paul assure us is happening in the inward man, according to 2 Corinthians 4:16?

    _____

    _____

For God so loved the
world . . .

NICODEMUS BEGINS with courtesies, "Teacher, we know you are a teacher sent from God, because no one can do the miracles you do unless God is with him" (John 3:2 NCV).

Jesus disregards the compliment. "I tell you the truth, unless you are born again, you cannot be in God's kingdom" (v. 3 NCV).

No chitchat here. No idle talk. Straight to the point. Straight to the heart. Straight to the problem.

You can't help the blind by turning up the light, Nicodemus.

You can't help the deaf by turning up the music, Nicodemus.

You can't change the inside by decorating the outside, Nicodemus.

You can't grow fruit without seed, Nicodemus.

You must be born again.

Whack! Whack! Whack!

The meeting between Jesus and Nicodemus was more than an encounter between two religious figures. It was a collision between two philosophies. Two opposing views on salvation.

Nicodemus thought the person did the work; Jesus says God does the work. Nicodemus thought it was a trade-off. Jesus says it is a gift. Nicodemus thought man's job was to earn it. Jesus says man's job is to accept it.

As Moses lifted up the serpent in the wilderness, even so must the Son of Man be lifted up, that whoever believes in Him should not perish but have eternal life.
JOHN 3:14–15

1. When is grace not grace, according to Romans 11:6?

_____

_____

_____

_____

2. Did you know Paul had a pedigree? He trots it out in Philippians 3:3–6:

Rejoicing, glorying in _____
   (the proper focus for all believers)

Not trusting _____
   (our own efforts to "do good")

Although having confidence in _____
   (I used to, you know)

More than others, having confidence in _____
   (let's compare notes, shall we?)

_____ when I was eight days old
   (obedient to the law from birth)

From the nation of _____
   (God's chosen people)

From the tribe of _____
   (the same as King Saul, his namesake)

A _____ of the _____
   (the best of the best, and proud of it)

Concerning the law, a _____
   (I knew the Scriptures inside out)

Persecuted the church because of my _____
   (my way needed to be protected)

Obeyed the law to the degree _____
   (no one could fault me).

3. Paul was one of the spiritual elite, but he traded his reputation away for something worth far more. What was his new perspective on that oh-so-impressive pedigree, according to Philippians 3:7–9?

_____

_____

_____

4. Man-made righteousness will always fall short. How does Isaiah 64:6 describe all our righteous deeds?

_____

_____

_____

A legalist believes the supreme force behind salvation is you. If you look right, speak right, and belong to the right segment of the right group, you will be saved. The brunt of responsibility doesn't lie within God; it lies within you.

> The result? The outside sparkles. The talk is good and the step is true. But look closely. Listen carefully. Something is missing. What is it? Joy. What's there? Fear. (That you won't do enough.) Arrogance. (That you have done enough.) Failure. (That you have made a mistake.)

5. If not works, then what? Paul's answer can be found in 2 Timothy 1:9.

_____

_____

_____

_____

Nicodemus knew how to march, but he longed to sing. He knew there was something more, but he didn't know where to find it. So he went to Jesus.
HE STILL MOVES STONES

6. Nicodemus is about to be introduced to the gospel of grace. We've heard it all before, but Jesus' words were about to knock this Pharisee's world off its axis.

___ Romans 3:24		a. Through grace, we are made rich.
___ Romans 5:2		b. God gives grace to the humble.
___ 2 Corinthians 8:9		c. Because of grace, we have hope.
___ Ephesians 2:8		d. By grace, we are freely justified, made right with God.
___ 2 Thessalonians 2:16		e. With Jesus, God's grace appeared to all.
___ 1 Timothy 1:14		f. We stand in grace.
___ Titus 2:11		g. God's grace is exceedingly abundant.
___ James 4:6		h. By grace we are saved through faith.

By now Nicodemus was growing edgy. Such light is too bright for his eyes. We religious teachers like to control and manage. We like to define and outline. Structure and clarity are the friend of the preacher. But they aren't always the protocol of God.

Salvation is God's business. Grace is his idea, his work, and his expense. He offers it to whom he desires, when he desires. Our job in the process is to inform the people, not to screen the people.

The question must have been written all over Nicodemus's face. Why would God do this? What would motivate him to offer such a gift? What Jesus told Nicodemus, Nicodemus never could have imagined. The motive behind the gift of new birth? Love. "God loved the world so much that he gave his one and only Son so that whoever believes in him may not be lost, but have eternal life" (John 3:16 NCV).

7. Grace is a gift of love. If Nicodemus was standing, he probably needed to take a seat about then. It wasn't a set of rules, a code of ethics, a twelve-step program, or a dress code. God gives us new birth because he loves us.

- How does Paul describe salvation's appearing in Titus 3:4–7?

_____

_____

_____

- Why does 1 John 4:9 say that God sent his Son?

_____

_____

_____

- What does God do with his love, according to Romans 5:5?

_____

_____

_____

8. What does Romans 8:38–39 teach us about the love of God?

_____

_____

_____

9. According to Mark 10:24, what term of tenderness does Jesus use for those who follow him?

_____

_____

But when the kindness and the love of God our Savior toward man appeared, not by works of righteousness which we have done, but according to His mercy He saved us, through the washing of regeneration and renewing of the Holy Spirit, whom He poured out on us abundantly through Jesus Christ our Savior, that having been justified by His grace we should become heirs according to the hope of eternal life.

TITUS 3:4–7

Nicodemus has never heard such words. Never. He has had many discussions of salvation. But this is the first in which no rules were given. No system was offered. No code or ritual. "Everyone who believes can have eternal life in him," Jesus told him. Could God be so generous? Even in the darkness of night, the amazement is seen on Nicodemus's face. *Everyone who believes can have eternal life.* Not "everyone who achieves." Not "everyone who succeeds." Not "everyone who agrees." But "everyone who believes."

Selections throughout this lesson were taken from *Just Like Jesus, In the Eye of the Storm, He Still Moves Stones,* and *When God Whispers Your Name.*

NOTES

NOTES

He's Astonishing

PICTURE SIX MEN walking on a narrow road. The gold dawn explodes behind them, stretching shadows ahead. Early-morning chill has robes snugly sashed. Grass sparkles with diamonds of dew.

The men's faces are eager, but common. Their leader is confident, but unknown. They call him Rabbi; he looks more like a laborer. And well he should, for he's spent far more time building than teaching. But this week the teaching has begun.

Where are they going? To the temple to worship? To the synagogue to teach? To the hills to pray? They haven't been told, but they each have their own idea.

John and Andrew expect to be led into the desert. That's where their previous teacher had taken them. John the Baptist would guide them into the barren hills, and for hours they would pray. For days they would fast. For the Messiah they would yearn. And now, the Messiah is here.

Surely he will do the same.

Everybody knows that a Messiah is a holy man. Everybody knows that self-denial is the first step to holiness. Surely

Now both Jesus and His disciples were invited to the wedding. And when they ran out of wine, the mother of Jesus said to Him, "They have no wine." Jesus said to her, "Woman, what does your concern have to do with Me? My hour has not yet come."
JOHN 2:2–4

God's voice is first heard by hermits. *Jesus is leading us into solitude.* At least that's what John and Andrew think.

Peter has another opinion. Peter is a man of action. A roll-up-your-sleeves kind of guy. A stand-up-and-say-it sort of fellow. He likes the idea of going somewhere. God's people need to be on the move. *Probably taking us somewhere to preach,* he is thinking to himself. And as they walk, Peter is outlining his own sermon, should Jesus need a breather.

Nathanael would disagree. *Come and see,* his friend Philip had invited. So he came. And Nathanael liked what he saw. In Jesus he saw a man of deep thought. A man of meditation. A heart of contemplation. A man who, like Nathanael, had spent hours under the fig tree reflecting on the mysteries of life. Nathanael was convinced that Jesus was taking them to a place to ponder. *A quiet house on a distant mountain—that's where we are going.*

And what about Philip? What was he thinking? He was the only apostle with a Gentile name. When the Greeks came looking for Jesus, it was Philip they approached. Perhaps he had Greek connections. Maybe Philip had a heart for Gentiles. If so, he was hoping this journey was a missionary one—out of Galilee. Out of Judea. Into a distant land.

Did such speculation occur? Who knows? I know it does today.

I know Jesus' followers often enlist with high aspirations and expectations. Disciples step in line with unspoken yet heartfelt agendas. Lips posed to preach to thousands. Eyes fixed on foreign shores. *I know where Jesus will take me,* the young disciples claim, and so they, like the first five, follow.

And they, like the first five, are surprised.

Maybe it was Andrew who asked it. Perhaps Peter. Could be that all approached Jesus. But I wager that at some point in the journey, the disciples expressed their assumptions.

"So, Rabbi, where are you taking us? To the desert?"

"No," opines another, "he's taking us to the temple."

"To the temple?" challenges a third. "We're on our way to the Gentiles!"

Then a chorus of confusion breaks out and ends only when Jesus lifts his hand and says softly, "We're on our way to a wedding."

Silence. John and Andrew look at each other. "A wedding?" they say. "John the Baptist would have never gone to a wedding. Why, there is drinking and laughter and dancing . . ."

"And noise!" Philip chimes in. "How can you meditate in a noisy wedding?"

"Or preach in a wedding?" Peter adds.

"Why would we go to a wedding?"

Good question. Why would Jesus, on his first journey, take his followers to a party? Didn't they have work to do? Didn't he have principles to teach? Wasn't his time limited? How could a wedding fit with his purpose on earth?

Why did Jesus go to the wedding?

The answer? It's found in the second verse of John 2. "Jesus and his followers were also invited to the wedding" (NCV).

1. When you think of "doing ministry," what do you see being accomplished? Is joy near the top of your to-do list?

_____

_____

_____

_____

2. David said, "You have put gladness in my heart" (Psalm 4:7). According to Psalm 97:11, what should be the attitude of those whose hearts are right with God?

_____

_____

_____

_____

3. The psalms are often songs of praise to the Lord. Consider which of the following statements have had particular meaning in your relationship with the Lord.

____ Those who trust God find reasons to rejoice. Those who love his name are joyful (Psalm 5:11).

____ Our gladness often finds expression through song (Psalm 9:2).

____ The fact that we have been saved brings a joy that can't be hidden. We must tell others (Psalm 9:14).

____ The righteous have reason to be glad, and that reason is the Lord (Psalm 32:11).

____ I'm so happy; my joy in the Lord is soul-deep (Psalm 35:9)!

4. This rejoicing is not one-sided. What picture of God do we see in Zephaniah 3:17?

_____

_____

_____

Serve the LORD with gladness; come before His presence with singing.

PSALM 100:2

5. Jesus was questioned because his followers were not fasting and praying. What answer did he give in Matthew 9:15?

_____

_____

_____

6. The Bible often compares our relationship with God to the one between a bride and her groom. What does Isaiah 62:5 tell us about God's feelings for his bride?

_____

_____

_____

When the bride and groom were putting the guest list together, Jesus' name was included. And when Jesus showed up with a half-dozen friends, the invitation wasn't rescinded. Whoever was hosting this party was happy to have Jesus present.

"Be sure and put Jesus' name on the list," he might have said. "He really lightens up a party."

Jesus wasn't invited because he was a celebrity. He wasn't one yet. The invitation wasn't motivated by his miracles. He'd yet to perform any. Why did they invite him?

I suppose they liked him.

Big deal? I think so. I think it's significant that common folk in a little town enjoyed being with Jesus. I think it's noteworthy that the Almighty didn't act high and mighty. The Holy One wasn't holier-than-thou. The One who knew it all wasn't a know-it-all. The One who made the stars didn't keep his head in them. The One who owns all the stuff of earth never strutted it.

7. What wedding are we all looking forward to, according to Revelation 19:7–9?

_____

_____

_____

DAY TWO
Give them something to eat . . .

When it was evening, His disciples came to Him, saying, "This is a deserted place, and the hour is already late. Send the multitudes away, that they may go into the villages and buy themselves food." But Jesus said to them, "They do not need to go away. You give them something to eat."

MATTHEW 14:15–16

WE HAVE EXPECTATIONS of God, but when pain comes into our world and these expectations go unmet, doubts may begin to surface.

We look for God, but can't find him. And now you aren't quite sure what you see.

The disciples weren't sure what they saw, either.

Jesus failed to meet their expectations. The day Jesus fed the five thousand men he didn't do what they wanted him to do. He sent them to the boat. Then he dismissed the crowd and ascended a mountainside. It was evening, probably around 6:00 p.m. The storm struck immediately. The sun had scarcely set before typhoon-like winds began to roar.

Note that Jesus sent the disciples out into the storm *alone.* Even as he was ascending the mountainside, he could feel and hear the gale's force. Jesus was not ignorant of the storm. He was aware that a torrent was coming that would carpet-bomb the sea's surface. But he didn't turn around. The disciples were left to face the storm . . . alone.

The greatest storm that night was not in the sky; it was in the disciples' hearts. The greatest fear was not from seeing the storm-driven waves; it came from seeing the back of their leader as he left them to face the night with only questions as companions.

It was this fury that the disciples were facing that night. Imagine the incredible strain of bouncing from wave to wave in a tiny fishing vessel. One hour would weary you. Two hours would exhaust you.

Surely Jesus will help us, they thought. They'd seen him still storms like this before. On this same sea, they had awakened him during a storm, and he had commanded the skies to be silent. They'd seen him quiet the wind and soothe the waves. *Surely he will come off the mountain.*

But he doesn't. Their arms begin to ache from rowing. Still no sign of Jesus. Three hours. Four hours. The winds rage. The boat bounces. Still no Jesus. Midnight comes. Their eyes search for God—in vain.

By now the disciples have been on the sea for as long as six hours.

All this time they have fought the storm and sought the Master. And, so far, the storm is winning. And the Master is nowhere to be found.

"Where is he?" cried one.

"Has he forgotten us?" yelled another.

"He feeds thousands of strangers and yet leaves us to die?" muttered a third.

The Gospel of Mark adds compelling insight into the disciples' attitude. "They had not understood about the loaves; their hearts were hardened" (Mark 6:52 NIV).

What does Mark mean? Simply this. The disciples were mad. They began the evening in a huff. Their hearts were hardened toward Jesus because he fed the multitude. Their preference, remember, had been to "send the crowds away" (Matthew 14:15 NIV). And Jesus had told them to feed the people. But they wouldn't try. They said it couldn't be done. They told Jesus to let the people take care of themselves.

But Jesus didn't. Instead, he chose to bypass the reluctant disciples and use the faith of an anonymous boy. What the disciples said couldn't be done was done—in spite of them, not through them.

1. It can be difficult to see God's plan when disappointment and doubts creep into our hearts.

 • What does Paul tell us about God's ways in Romans 11:33?

 _____

 _____

 _____

- What comfort can you draw from the truth of Romans 8:28?

_____

_____

_____

- Why does it help to remember Joseph's words in Genesis 50:20?

_____

_____

_____

2. The Lord is also asking you to feed the people. Give a few examples of specific ways you can accomplish this in your own life.

_____

_____

_____

The disciples pouted. They sulked. Rather than being amazed at the miracle, they became mad at the Master. After all, they had felt foolish passing out the very bread they said could not be made. Add to that Jesus' command to go to the boat when they wanted to go to battle, and it's easier to understand why these guys are burning!

"Now what is Jesus up to, leaving us out on the sea on a night like this?"

It's 1:00 a.m., no Jesus.

It's 2:00 a.m., no Jesus.

Peter, Andrew, James, and John have seen storms like this. They are fishermen; the sea is their life. They know the havoc the gale-force winds can wreak. They've seen the splintered hulls float to shore. They've attended the funerals. They know, better than anyone, that this night could be their last. "Why doesn't he come?" they sputter.

Finally, he does. "During the fourth watch of the night [3:00 to 6:00 a.m.] Jesus went out to them, walking on the lake" (Matthew 14:25 NIV).

Jesus came. He finally came. But between verse 24—the boat being buffeted by waves—and verse 25—when Jesus appeared—a thousand questions are asked.

Questions you have probably asked, too. Perhaps you know the angst of being suspended between verses 24 and 25. Maybe you're riding a storm, searching the coastline for a light, a glimmer of hope. You know that Jesus knows what you are going through. You know that he's aware of your storm. But as hard as you look to find him, you can't see him. Maybe your heart, like the disciples' hearts, has been hardened by unmet expectations. Your pleadings for help are salted with angry questions.

3. What does James 1:5–7 say about doubt?

_____

_____

_____

4. Put 1 Timothy 1:18–19 into your own words in the space below.

_____

_____

_____

_____

5. The Lord asks for our trust, even when the path before us seems as impossible as a wind-tossed sea. What does Solomon remind us in Proverbs 3:5?

_____

_____

_____

6. What promise is found in Psalm 37:5–6?

_____

_____

_____

The message? When you can't see him, trust him. The figure you see is not a ghost. The voice you hear is not the wind.

Jesus is closer than you've ever dreamed. ✳

FAITH IS often the child of fear.

Fear propelled Peter out of the boat. He'd ridden these waves before. He knew what these storms could do. He'd heard the stories. He'd seen the wreckage. He knew the widows. He knew the storm could kill. And he wanted out.

All night he wanted out. For nine hours he'd tugged on sails, wrestled with oars, and searched every shadow on the horizon for hope. He was soaked to the soul and bone weary of the wind's banshee wail.

Look into Peter's eyes and you won't see a man of conviction. Search his face and you won't find a gutsy grimace. Later on, you will. You'll see his courage in the garden. You'll witness his devotion at Pentecost. You'll behold his faith in his epistles.

But not tonight. Look into his eyes tonight and see fear—a suffocating, heart-racing fear of a man who has no way out.

But out of this fear would be born an act of faith, for faith is often the child of fear.

"The fear of the LORD is the beginning of wisdom," wrote the wise man (Proverbs 9:10 NIV).

Peter could have been his sermon illustration.

If Peter had seen Jesus walking on the water during a calm, peaceful day, do you think that he would have walked out to him?

Nor do I.

And when the disciples saw Him walking on the sea, they were troubled, saying, "It is a ghost!" And they cried out for fear.
MATTHEW 14:26

Had the lake been carpet smooth and the journey pleasant, do you think that Peter would have begged Jesus to take him on a stroll across the top of the water? Doubtful.

But give a man a choice between sure death and a crazy chance, and he'll take the chance . . . every time.

Great acts of faith are seldom born out of calm calculation.

1. What does Job 28:28 say about the part that fear plays in our lives?

_____

_____

_____

2. Scripture tells us that godly fear is a good thing—"serve God acceptably with reverence and godly fear" (Hebrews 12:28). Why does Luke 12:5 say we should have this attitude?

_____

_____

_____

3. On the other hand, because God is with us, we don't have to be fearful of everything else. What do these verses say we don't have to fear?

   • Proverbs 1:33

_____

_____

   • Psalm 46:1–2

_____

_____

- Isaiah 51:7

  _____

  _____

- Psalm 23:4

  _____

  _____

At the beginning of every act of faith, there is often a seed of fear. Fear of death. Fear of failure. Fear of loneliness. Fear of a wasted life. Fear of failing to know God.

IN THE EYE OF THE STORM

4. When faced with a choice between the relative safety of his pitching craft and a place at Jesus' side, Peter was ready to take a leap of faith—right over the side of the boat. What is God's message for the fearful-hearted in Isaiah 35:4?

   _____

   _____

   _____

5. Peter counted on the fact that his Lord would hold him up. It's a promise that had been made before. Write out Isaiah 41:10 in the space below.

   _____

   _____

   _____

For God has not given us a spirit of fear, but of power and of love and of a sound mind.

2 TIMOTHY 1:7

6. God doesn't promise only to hold us up. What _else_ does he promise to hold, according to Isaiah 41:13?

   _____

   _____

   _____

7. What is God, according to Hebrew 13:6?

_____

_____

_____

Faith is a desperate dive
out of the sinking boat of
human effort and a prayer
that God will be there to
pull us out of the water.

IN THE EYE OF THE STORM

We, like Peter, are aware of two facts: We are going down and God is standing up. So we scramble out. We leave behind the *Titanic* of self-righteousness and stand on the solid path of God's grace.

And, surprisingly, we are able to walk on water. Death is disarmed. Failures are forgivable. Life has real purpose. And God is not only within sight; he is within reach.

With precious, wobbly steps, we draw closer to him. For a season of surprising strength, we stand upon his promises. It doesn't make sense that we are able to do this. We don't claim to be worthy of such an incredible gift. When people ask how in the world we can keep our balance during such stormy times, we don't boast. We don't brag. We point unabashedly to the One who makes it possible. Our eyes are on him. ✳

Take courage . . .

SUPPOSE ONE OF JESUS' DISCIPLES kept a journal. And suppose that disciple made an entry in the journal on the morning after the storm. And suppose we discovered that journal. Here is how it would read . . . I suppose.

Only minutes before, chaos had erupted.

Oh, how the storm roared. Stars were hidden by a black ceiling. Clouds billowed like smoke. Bolts of lightning were the conductor's baton that cued the kettledrums of thunder to rumble.

And rumble they did. The clouds seemed to rise as a bear on hind legs and growl. The booms shook everything: the heavens, the earth, and—most of all—the sea. It was as if the Sea of Galilee were a bowl in the hands of a dancing giant. From the bowels of the lake the waves came, turning the glassy surface into a mountain range of snow-topped waves. Five, ten, even fifteen feet into the air they mounted, rising and falling like swallows chasing mosquitoes.

In the midst of the sea, our boat bounced. The waves slapped it as easily as children would a ball. Our straining at the oars scarcely budged it. We were at the storm's mercy. The waves lifted us up so high that we felt like we were in midair. Then down into the valley we plunged.

We were a twig in a whirlpool . . . a leaf in the wind. We were helpless.

That's when the light appeared. At first I thought it was a reflection of the moon, a gleam on the surface of the water. But the night held no moon. I looked again. The light was

Immediately Jesus spoke to them, saying, "Be of good cheer! It is I; do not be afraid."
MATTHEW 14:27

moving toward us, not over the waves but through them. I wasn't the only one who saw it.

"A ghost," someone screamed. Fear of the sea was eclipsed by a new terror. Thoughts raced as the specter drew near. *Was it a figment of our imagination? Was it a vision? Who? How? What was this mystical light that appeared so . . . ?*

A flash of lightning illuminated the sky. For a second I could see its face . . . his face. A second was all I needed.

It was the Master!

He spoke: "Take courage! It is I. Don't be afraid" (Matthew 14:27 NIV).

Nothing had changed. The storm still raged. The wind still shrieked. The boat still pitched. The thunder still boomed. The rain still slapped. But in the midst of the tumult, I could hear his voice. Although he was still far away, it was like he was by my side. The night was ferocious, yet he spoke as though the sea were placid and the sky silent.

And, somehow, courage came.

"Lord, if it's you . . . tell me to come to you on the water" (v. 28 NIV).

The voice was Peter's. He wasn't being cocky. He wasn't demanding proof. He was scared. Like me, he knew what this storm could do. He knew that the boat would soon go down. He knew that Jesus was standing up. And he knew where he wanted to be . . . where we all wanted to be.

1. Somewhere between fear and faith, we must find courage. Scripture tells us where to look for it.

   • According to Deuteronomy 31:6, why can a child of God have courage?

   _____

   _____

- What does Joshua 1:9 say, and why?

_____

_____

- In Psalm 27:14, what is promised?

_____

_____

2. Peter was faced with what seemed impossible, yet he was willing to step over the side of the boat and go to the Lord's side. Where does Proverbs 3:5 encourage us to place our trust? What is our other option?

_____

_____

_____

_____

3. The call to trust can be found throughout the Bible.

___ Psalm 31:14	a. Our trust in God should be everlasting.
___ Psalm 36:7	b. God gives peace to those who trust him.
___ Isaiah 26:3	c. God knows those who trust in him.
___ Isaiah 26:4	d. We must trust in God, not in ourselves.
___ Jeremiah 17:7	e. I trust God because he is my God.
___ Nahum 1:7	f. Those who trust God are called blessed.
___ 2 Corinthians 1:9	g. We trust God in part because of his love.

4. According to Psalm 9:10, what has the Lord never done?

_____

_____

_____

"Come on," Jesus invited.

So Peter climbed over the side and stepped onto the sea. Before him opened a trail through a forest of waves. He stepped quickly. Water splashed. But he kept going. This path to Jesus was a ribbon of calm. It was peaceful. Serene.

Jesus radiated light at the end of the trail. Smiling.

Peter stepped toward the light like it was his only hope. He was halfway there when we all heard the thunder. It boomed, and he stopped. I saw his head turn. He looked up at the sky. He looked up at the clouds. He felt the wind. And down he went.

Boy did he yell!

A hand came through the water sheets and grabbed Peter. Lightning flashed again, and I could see the face of Jesus. I noticed that his smile was gone. Hurt covered his face. It was like he couldn't believe that we couldn't believe. Danger to us was just a detour to him. I wanted to ask him, "Aren't you afraid, Jesus? Aren't you afraid?"

But I said nothing. Before I knew it, he was in the boat with us.

The sea stilled as silk.

The winds hushed.

A canyon opened in the clouds; soft moonlight fell over the water.

It happened instantaneously. It didn't take the rest of the night. It didn't take an hour. It didn't take a minute. It happened in a blink.

From chaos to calm. From panic to peace. The sky was so suddenly silent that I could hear my heart pounding. I thought I was dreaming. Then I saw the wide eyes of the others and felt my clothing soaked against my skin. This was no dream. I looked at the water. I looked at Peter. I looked at the others. And then I looked at him.

And I did the only thing I could have done. With the stars as my candles and the stilled boat as my altar, I fell at his feet and worshiped.

5. What does Jesus invite his followers to do in John 14:1?

_____

_____

_____

Watch, stand fast in the faith, be brave, be strong.

1 CORINTHIANS 16:13

6. Later, in Matthew 21:21, what does Jesus tell his disciples about faith?

_____

_____

_____

7. What did the disciples request of the Lord in Luke 17:5?

_____

_____

_____

8. Faith isn't characterized by unsteady seas and tossing waves. What does Paul say about our faith in Colossians 1:23?

_____

_____

_____

There are times in a person's life when, even in the midst of them, you know you'll never be the same. Moments that forever serve as journey posts. This was one.

I had never seen Jesus as I saw him then. I had seen him as powerful. I had seen him as wise. I had witnessed his authority and marveled at his abilities. But what I witnessed last night, I know I'll never forget.

I saw God. The God who can't sit still when the storm is too strong. The God who lets me get frightened enough to need him and then comes close enough for me to see him. The God who uses my storms as his path to come to me.

I saw God. It took a storm for me to see him. But I saw him. And I'll never be the same. ✳

MARTHA HAD HOPED Jesus would show up to heal Lazarus. He didn't. Then she'd hoped he'd show up to bury Lazarus. He didn't. By the time he made it to Bethany, Lazarus was four-days buried, and Martha was wondering what kind of friend Jesus was.

Then Jesus, again groaning in Himself, came to the tomb. It was a cave, and a stone lay against it. Jesus said, "Take away the stone."
JOHN 11:38–39

She hears he's at the edge of town so she storms out to meet him. "Lord, if you had been here," she confronts, "my brother would not have died" (John 11:21 NCV).

There is hurt in those words. Hurt and disappointment. The one man who could have made a difference didn't, and Martha wants to know why.

Maybe you do, too. Maybe you've done what Martha did. Someone you love ventures near the edge of life, and you turn to Jesus for help. You, like Martha, turn to the only one who can pull a person from the ledge of death. You ask Jesus to give a hand.

Martha must have thought, *Surely he will come. Didn't he aid the paralytic? Didn't he help the leper? Didn't he give sight to the blind? And they hardly knew Jesus. Lazarus is his friend. We're like family. Doesn't Jesus come for the weekend? Doesn't he eat at our table? When he hears that Lazarus is sick, he'll be here in a heartbeat.*

But he didn't come. Lazarus got worse. She watched out the window. Jesus didn't show. Her brother drifted in and out of consciousness. "He'll be here soon, Lazarus," she promised. "Hang on."

But the knock at the door never came. Jesus never appeared. Not to help. Not to heal. Not to bury. And now, four days later, he finally shows up. The funeral is over. The body is buried, and the grave is sealed.

And Martha is hurt.

Her words have been echoed in a thousand cemeteries. "If you had been here, my brother would not have died."

The grave unearths our view of God.

When we face death, our definition of God is challenged. Which, in turn, challenges our faith. Which leads me to ask a grave question. Why is it that we interpret the presence of death as the absence of God? Why do we think that if the body is not healed, then God is not near? Is healing the only way God demonstrates his presence?

Sometimes we think so. And as a result, when God doesn't answer our prayers for healing, we get angry. Resentful. Blame replaces belief. "If you had been here, doing your part, God, then this death would not have happened."

It's distressing that this view of God has no place for death.

1. Death came into the world as a result of sin. What did God tell Adam in Genesis 3:19?

_____

_____

_____

2. Eternity is vast, and in comparison our lives are fleeting. Look up the following verses, and describe what they're saying:

• Job 14:1–2

_____

_____

For when a few years are finished, I shall go the way of no return.

—JOB 16:22

- Psalm 90:9

  _____

  _____

- James 4:14

  _____

  _____

3. The presence of death in this world doesn't mean God is not with us. Quite the contrary. Take a look at the one the Lord declares as his enemy.

   Hosea 13:14 – What will the Lord do to death? What will death lose?

   _____

   _____

   _____

   1 Corinthians 15:26 – How is death described? What will happen to death?

   _____

   _____

   _____

Physical death isn't something to be feared, and it doesn't stand in the Lord's way. Please understand, Jesus didn't raise the dead for the sake of the dead. He raised the dead for the sake of the living.

"Lazarus, come out!" (John 11:43 NCV).

Martha was silent as Jesus commanded. The mourners were quiet. No one stirred as Jesus stood face to face with the rock-hewn tomb and demanded that it release his friend.

No one stirred, that is, except for Lazarus. Deep within the tomb, he moved. His stilled heart began to beat again.

Wrapped eyes popped open. Wooden fingers lifted. And a mummied man in a tomb sat up. And want to know what happened next?

Let John tell you. "The dead man came out, his hands and feet wrapped with pieces of cloth, and a cloth around his face" (v. 44 NCV).

Question: What kind of God is this?

Answer: The God who holds the keys to life and death.

The kind of God you want present at your funeral.

4. Take a look for yourself. What does Jesus declare in Revelation 1:18?

_____

_____

_____

5. Jesus conquered death, but not just *physical* death.

- What kind of death does Paul describe in Ephesians 2:5?

_____

_____

- What does 2 Timothy 1:10 say?

_____

_____

- What does Jesus himself say in John 5:24–25?

_____

_____

6. Our lives have undergone a shift—from ephemeral to eternal. How does Paul describe this transformation in Colossians 2:13?

_____

_____

_____

He'll do it again, you know. He's promised he would. And he's shown that he can.

> "The Lord himself will come down from heaven with a loud command" (1 Thessalonians 4:16 NCV).

> The same voice that awoke the boy near Nain, that stirred the still daughter of Jairus, that awakened the corpse of Lazarus—the same voice will speak again. The earth and the sea will give up their dead. There will be no more death.

> Jesus made sure of that.

7. What does Romans 6:9 tell us about Jesus and death?

_____

_____

_____

8. What do we have to look forward to, according to Revelation 21:4?

_____

_____

_____

※

Selections throughout this lesson were taken from *When God Whispers Your Name*, *In the Eye of the Storm*, and *He Still Moves Stones*.

Our Savior Jesus Christ . . . has abolished death and brought life and immortality to light through the gospel.
—2 TIMOTHY 1:10

NOTES

NOTES

NOTES

LESSON THREE

He's Teaching

DAY ONE
All authority has
been given to me . . .

YOU HAVE TO ADMIT some of our hearts are trashed out. Let any riffraff knock on the door, and we throw it open. Anger shows up, and we let him in. Revenge needs a place to stay, so we have him pull up a chair. Pity wants to have a party, so we show him the kitchen. Lust rings the bell, and we change the sheets on the bed. Don't we know how to say no?

Many don't. For most of us, thought management is, well, unthought of. We think much about time management, weight management, personnel management, even scalp management. But what about thought management? Shouldn't we be as concerned about managing our thoughts as we are about managing anything else? Jesus was. Like a trained soldier at the gate of a city, he stood watch over his mind. He stubbornly guarded the gateway of his heart. Many thoughts were denied entrance. Need an example?

How about arrogance? On one occasion the people determined to make Jesus their king. What an attractive thought. Most of us would delight in the notion of royalty.

And Jesus came and spoke to them, saying, "All authority has been given to Me in heaven and on earth."
MATTHEW 28:18

Even if we refused the crown, we would enjoy considering the invitation. Not Jesus. "Jesus saw that in their enthusiasm, they were about to grab him and make him king, so he slipped off and went back up the mountain to be by himself" (John 6:15 MSG).

1. What advice did King David give to his son Solomon, according to 1 Chronicles 28:9?

   _____

   _____

   _____

2. In his turn, Solomon did the urging. What does Proverbs 16:3 command? What will be the consequence?

   _____

   _____

   _____

3. Which of these scriptural truths can you apply to your own walk of faith?

   ___ It's wise to observe how faithful followers live their lives (Hebrews 12:1).

   ___ The greatest source of joy is found in what is unseen (1 Peter 1:8).

   ___ Since God's love is made perfect in us, we can show his compassion by helping others (1 John 3:16–18).

   ___ Challenges are a fact of life, but a faithful heart always has hope (Romans 12:12).

4. Even when we make thought management a priority, we let our guard slip, and sin enters. What encouragement can we find in the words of Isaiah 55:7?

_____

_____

_____

5. What promise does the wise man give in Proverbs 22:5?

_____

_____

_____

Jesus guarded his heart. If he did, shouldn't we do the same? Most certainly! "Be careful what you think, because your thoughts run your life" (Proverbs 4:23 NCV). Jesus wants your heart to be fertile and fruitful. He wants you to have a heart like his. That is God's goal for you. He wants you to "think and act like Christ Jesus" (Philippians 2:5 NCV). But how? The answer is surprisingly simple. We can be transformed if we make one decision: *I will submit my thoughts to the authority of Jesus.*

6. What does each of these verses teach us about guarding our hearts?

- Proverbs 13:6

_____

_____

- 2 Thessalonians 3:3

_____

_____

Thorns and snares are in the way of the perverse; he who guards his soul will be far from them.

PROVERBS 22:5

• Philippians 4:7

_____

_____

It's easy to overlook a significant claim made by Christ at the conclusion of Matthew's gospel. "All authority in heaven and on earth has been given to me" (Matthew 28:18 NIV). Jesus claims to be the CEO of heaven and earth. He has the ultimate say on everything, especially our thoughts. He has more authority, for example, than your parents. Your parents may say you are no good, but Jesus says you are valuable, and he has authority over parents. He even has more authority over you than you do. You may tell yourself that you are too bad to be forgiven, but Jesus has a different opinion. If you give him authority over you, then your guilty thoughts are no longer allowed.

7. What are the thoughts of our Lord toward us, according to Jeremiah 29:11?

_____

_____

8. Jesus was given authority over heaven and earth—that's on the grand scale. But he also has authority over his own—you and me. What do we learn about this earth's CEO from the following verses? Match them up.

____ Matthew 7:28–29   a. Jesus has the authority to give eternal life.

____ John 3:35   b. Jesus has the authority to judge.

____ John 5:26–27   c. Jesus is under his Father's authority.

____ John 14:10   d. Jesus taught with authority.

____ John 17:1–2   e. In the end, everyone will acknowledge Jesus' authority.

____ Philippians 2:9–11   f. God gave all things into Jesus' hand.

Jesus also has authority over your ideas. Suppose you have an idea that you want to rob a grocery store. Jesus, however, has made it clear that stealing is wrong. If you have given him authority over your ideas, then the idea of stealing cannot remain in your thoughts.

See what I mean by authority? To have a pure heart, we must submit all thoughts to the authority of Christ. If we are willing to do that, he will change us to be like him. ✳

DAY TWO

He who has ears, let him hear . . .

He who has ears to hear,
let him hear!
MATTHEW 11:15

"LET HE who has ears to hear, use them."

More than once Jesus said these words. Eight times in the Gospels and eight times in the Book of Revelation,[1] we are reminded that it's not enough just to have ears—it's necessary to use them.

In one of his parables,[2] Jesus compared our ears to soil. He told about a farmer who scattered seed (symbolic of the Word) in four different types of ground (symbolic of our ears). Some of our ears are like a hard road—unreceptive to the seed. Others have ears like rocky soil—we hear the Word but don't allow it to take root. Still others have ears akin to a weed patch—too overgrown, too thorny, with too much competition for the seed to have a chance. And then there are some who have ears that hear: well tilled, discriminate, and ready to hear God's voice.

Please note that in all four cases the seed is the same seed. The sower is the same sower. What's different is not the message or the messenger—it's the listener. And if the ratio in the story is significant, three-fourths of the world isn't listening to God's voice. Whether the cause be hard hearts, shallow lives, or anxious minds, 75 percent of us are missing the message.

It's not that we don't have ears; it's that we don't use them.

1. What are we wise to do, according to Proverbs 18:15?

_____

_____

_____

_____

2. We can learn just as much from negative examples—seeing how *not* to live—as from positive ones. Consider these verses, which are heavy on chastisement.

____ Mark 8:18   a. Foolish people hear without understanding.

____ Isaiah 42:20   b. Dull-hearted people shut their eyes.

____ Isaiah 6:10   c. Stiff-necked and stubborn people resist the Holy Spirit.

____ Jeremiah 5:21   d. The disciples did not see, hear, or remember.

____ Acts 7:51   e. The "blind" see without observing, without paying attention.

3. On the other hand, some have ears that are ready to listen. What does Isaiah 30:21 say that these people will have?

_____

_____

_____

Scripture has always placed a premium on hearing God's voice. Indeed, the great command from God through Moses began with the words "Hear, O Israel: the LORD our God is one LORD" (Deuteronomy 6:4 KJV).

Nehemiah and his men were commended because they were "attentive unto the book of the law" (Nehemiah 8:3 KJV).

"Happy are those who listen to me" is the promise of Proverbs 8:34 (NCV). Jesus urges us to learn to listen like sheep. "The sheep recognize his voice. . . . and they follow because they are familiar with [the shepherd's] voice. They won't follow a stranger's voice but will scatter because they aren't used to the sound of it" (John 10:3–5 MSG).

Each of the seven churches in Revelation is addressed in the same manner: "He who has an ear, let him hear what the Spirit says to the churches."[3]

Our ears, unlike our eyes, do not have lids. They are to remain open, but how easily they close.

4. The Lord says, "Incline your ears to the words of my mouth" (Psalm 78:1). Though his people could be stubborn, God never stopped calling out to them.

- What would God delight to find, according to Isaiah 32:3?

  _____

  _____

- In Ezekiel 3:10, what does God ask for?

  _____

  _____

5. Who does the Lord call blessed in Matthew 13:16?

  _____

  _____

  _____

6. What word of caution is found in 2 Timothy 4:3?

_____

_____

_____

"Let he who has ears to hear, use them." How long has it been since you had your hearing checked? When God throws seed your way, what is the result? May I raise a question or two to test how well you hear God's voice?

How long has it been since you let God have you?

I mean really *have* you? How long since you gave him a portion of undiluted, uninterrupted time listening for his voice? Apparently Jesus did. He made a deliberate effort to spend time with God.

Spend much time reading about the listening life of Jesus and a distinct pattern emerges. He spent regular time with God, praying and listening. Mark says, "Very early in the morning, while it was still dark, Jesus got up, left the house and went off to a solitary place, where he prayed" (Mark 1:35 NIV). Luke tells us, "Jesus often withdrew to lonely places and prayed" (Luke 5:16 NIV).

Let me ask the obvious. If Jesus, the Son of God, the sinless Savior of humankind, thought it worthwhile to clear his calendar to pray, wouldn't we be wise to do the same? ✳

NOT ONLY did Jesus spend regular time with God in prayer, he spent regular time in God's Word. Of course we don't find Jesus pulling a leather-bound New Testament from his satchel and reading it. We do, however, see the stunning example of Jesus, in the throes of the wilderness temptation, using the Word of God to deal with Satan. Three times he is tempted, and each time he repels the attack with Scripture as his authority (Luke 4:4, 8, 12). Jesus is so familiar with Scripture that he not only knows the verse; he knows how to use it.

And then there's the occasion when Jesus is asked to read in the synagogue. He is handed the book of Isaiah the prophet. He finds the passage, reads it, and declares, "While you heard these words just now, they were coming true!" (Luke 4:21 NCV). We are given the picture of a person who knows his way around in Scripture and can recognize its fulfillment. If Jesus thought it wise to grow familiar with the Bible, shouldn't we do the same?

If we are to be just like Jesus—if we are to have ears that hear God's voice—then we have just found two habits worth imitating: the habits of prayer and Bible reading.

1. Paul tells us that "through Him we both have access by one Spirit to the Father" (Ephesians 2:18). Since God welcomes our prayers, how does Hebrews 10:19 say we should come before the Father?

_____

_____

_____

2. When we speak to God, he promises to hear our prayer.

- What does Psalm 10:17 say God does in response to us?

_____

_____

_____

- What promise do we find in Isaiah 65:24?

_____

_____

_____

3. How often are we encouraged to pray by Paul in Ephesians 6:18? How is this possible?

_____

_____

_____

4. What good can prayer do? What does James 5:16 say?

_____

_____

_____

_____

Wait a minute. Don't you do that. I know exactly what some of you are doing. You are tuning me out. *Lucado is talking about daily devotionals, eh? This is a good time for me to take a mental walk over to the fridge and see what we have to eat.*

I understand your reluctance. Some of us have tried to have a daily quiet time and have not been successful. Others of us have a hard time concentrating. And all of us are busy. So rather than spend time with God, listening for his voice, we'll let others spend time with him and then benefit from their experience. Let them tell us what God is saying. After all, isn't that why we pay preachers? Isn't that why we read Christian books? *These folks are good at daily devotions. I'll just learn from them.*

If that is your approach, if your spiritual experiences are secondhand and not firsthand, I'd like to challenge you with this thought: Do you do that with other parts of your life? I don't think so.

You don't do that with vacations. You don't say, "Vacations are such a hassle, packing bags and traveling. I'm going to send someone on vacation for me. When he returns, I'll hear all about it and be spared all the inconvenience." Would you do that? No! You want the experience firsthand. You want the sights firsthand, and you want to rest firsthand. Certain things no one can do for you.

5. Consider for a few verses just what it is you hold in your hands when you open your Bible:

- Why does the beloved disciple say he wrote his gospel, according to John 20:31?

_____

_____

- What does Acts 20:32 say about God's Word?

_____

_____

- How many reasons can you find to be amazed by the Scriptures in 2 Timothy 3:16–17?

_____

From childhood you have known the Holy Scriptures, which are able to make you wise for salvation through faith which is in Christ Jesus.

2 TIMOTHY 3:15

6. God's Word is "living and powerful" (Hebrews 4:12), and we need to search it out for ourselves. These verses encourage us to do just that. Match the verse with its message.

____ Deuteronomy 8:3   a. Search and read the Scriptures.

____ 1 Chronicles 28:8   b. The Law and the Prophets are true.

____ Psalm 119:140   c. Listen to those who teach God's Word.

____ Isaiah 34:16   d. Be careful to seek out and obey God's commands.

____ Malachi 2:7   e. We need the Word more than food.

____ John 5:46   f. The Scripture cannot be broken; it cannot be false.

____ John 10:35   g. The Word of God is pure; it has been tested.

____ Acts 24:14   h. Moses wrote about the coming Messiah.

7. What efforts will God bless, according to James 1:25?

_____

_____

_____

8. What word of caution can be found for students of the Scriptures in 2 Peter 1:20–21?

_____

_____

> The man who looks into the perfect law, the law of liberty, and makes a habit of so doing, is not the man who hears and forgets. He puts that law into practice and he wins true happiness.
>
> JAMES 1:25 PHILLIPS

9. When we look to the Word, praying for understanding as we read, study, and ponder our way through its pages, what will come to pass, according to Colossians 3:16?

_____

_____

_____

Listening to God is a firsthand experience. When he asks for your attention, God doesn't want you to send a substitute; he wants you. He wants to spend time with you. And with a little training, your time with God can be the highlight of your day. ✳

GOD SPEAKS to us through his Word. The first step in reading the Bible is to ask God to help you understand it. "But the Helper will teach you everything and will cause you to remember all that I told you. This Helper is the Holy Spirit whom the Father will send in my name" (James 14:26 NCV).

Before reading the Bible, pray. Don't go to Scripture looking for your own idea; go searching for God's. Read the Bible prayerfully. Also, read the Bible carefully. Jesus told us, "Search, and you will find" (Matthew 7:7 NCV). God commends those who "chew on Scripture day and night" (Psalm 1:2 MSG). The Bible is not a newspaper to be skimmed but rather a mine to be quarried. "Search for it like silver, and hunt for it like hidden treasure. Then you will understand respect for the LORD, and you will find that you know God" (Proverbs 2:4–5 NCV).

But the Helper, the Holy Spirit, whom the Father will send in My name, He will teach you all things, and bring to your remembrance all things that I said to you.
JOHN 14:26

1. Jesus promised to send a Helper. What does each of these verses say that the Holy Spirit would do once he arrived?

  • John 14:16

  _____

  _____

  • John 14:26

  _____

  _____

- John 15:26

_____

_____

- John 16:13

_____

_____

- John 16:14

_____

_____

His Holy Spirit, moving and breathing in you, is the most intimate part of your life, making you fit for himself. Don't take such a gift for granted.

EPHESIANS 4:30 MSG

2. Jesus was filled with the Spirit. How does Isaiah 11:2 describe the "help" he provides?

_____

_____

3. What else did we receive when we were given the Holy Spirit, according to 1 Corinthians 2:12–13?

_____

_____

_____

4. What insight is the Spirit able to provide, according to 1 Corinthians 2:9–10?

_____

_____

_____

5. In 1 John 2:27, how is the Spirit's role described?

_____

_____

_____

Here is a practical point. Study the Bible a little at a time. God seems to send messages as he did his manna: one day's portion at a time. He provides "a command here, a command there. A rule here, a rule there. A little lesson here, a little lesson there" (Isaiah 28:10 NCV). Choose depth over quantity. Read until a verse "hits" you, then stop and meditate on it. Copy the verse onto a sheet of paper, or write it in your journal, and reflect on it several times.

> On the morning I wrote this, for example, my quiet time found me in Matthew 18. I was only four verses into the chapter when I read, "The greatest person in the kingdom of heaven is the one who makes himself humble like this child." I needed to go no further. I copied the words in my journal and have pondered them on and off during the day. Several times I asked God, "How can I be more childlike?" By the end of the day, I was reminded of my tendency to hurry and my proclivity to worry.

6. We know that gaining wisdom is a good thing. How do we acquire wisdom, according to Proverbs 2:1–6?

_____

_____

_____

_____

Turn at my rebuke; surely I will pour out my spirit on you; I will make my words known to you.

PROVERBS 1:23

7. "Who has put wisdom in the mind? Or who has given understanding to the heart?" (Job 38:36). Time and again, Scripture tells us where to turn.

___ Psalm 119:73   a. Those who desire more of the Word will grow.

___ Psalm 119:99   b. The Lord speaks knowledge and understanding.

___ Proverbs 2:3–5   c. We gain insight from meditating on God's testimonies, his statutes.

___ Proverbs 2:6   d. The Spirit helps us to keep God's statutes.

___ James 1:5   e. The One who made us gives us understanding.

___ Ezekiel 36:27   f. The Lord gives understanding in all things.

___ 2 Timothy 2:7   g. If we cry out for understanding, we will gain a knowledge of God.

___ 1 Peter 2:2   h. God is the source of wisdom.

8. Take a look at these two verses from the Gospel of Luke. When do they take place in the scope of Jesus' life here on earth? What is he doing in each?

• Luke 2:47

_____

_____

_____

• Luke 24:45

_____

_____

_____

9. What is Paul's prayer for believers in Ephesians 1:18?

_____

_____

_____

Will I learn what God intends? If I listen, I will.

Don't be discouraged if your reading reaps a small harvest. Some days a lesser portion is all we need. A little girl returned from her first day at school. Her mom asked, "Did you learn anything?" "I guess not," the girl responded. "I have to go back tomorrow and the next day and the next day . . ."

Such is the case with learning. And such is the case with Bible study. Understanding comes a little at a time over a lifetime. ❋

*Now behold, two of them
were traveling that same
day to a village called
Emmaus, which was
seven miles from
Jerusalem. And they
talked together of all
these things which
had happened.*
LUKE 24:13–14

DESPAIR NOT ONLY clouds our vision; it hardens our hearts. We get cynical. We get calloused. And when good news comes, we don't want to accept it for fear of being disappointed again. That's what happened to two disciples on the road to Emmaus.

As they walk, they talk "about everything that had happened" (Luke 24:14 NCV). It's not hard to imagine their words.

"Why did the people turn against him?"

"He could have come down from the cross. Why didn't he?"

"He just let Pilate push him around."

"What do we do now?"

Later on they say these words: "And today some women among us amazed us. Early this morning they went to the tomb, but they did not find his body there. They came and told us that they had seen a vision of angels who said that Jesus was alive! So some of our group went to the tomb, too. They found it just as the women said, but they did not see Jesus" (Luke 24:22–24 NCV).

When reading Scripture, we can't always tell in what tone the words were spoken. Sometimes we don't know if the speaker means to be jubilant or sad or peaceful. This time, however, there is no question about what they're thinking: *As if it's not bad enough that Jesus was killed, now some grave robber has taken the body and duped some of our friends.*

These two followers aren't about to believe the women. Fool me once, shame on you. Fool me twice, shame on me.

Cleopas and his friend are putting their hearts in a shell. They won't take another risk. They won't be hurt again.

Common reaction—isn't it? Been hurt by love? Then don't love. Had a promise violated? Then don't trust. Had your heart broken? Then don't give it away.

There is a line, a fine line, which once crossed can be fatal. It's the line between disappointment and anger. Between hurt and hate, between bitterness and blame. If you are nearing that line, let me urge you, don't cross it. Step back and ask this question: How long am I going to pay for my disappointment? How long am I going to go on nursing my hurt?

At some point you have to move on. At some point you have to heal. At some point you have to let Jesus do for you what he did for these men.

Know what he did? First of all, he came to them. He didn't sit back and cross his arms and say, "Why can't those two get with the program?" He didn't complain to the angel and say, "Why won't they believe the empty tomb? Why are they so hard to please?"

What did he do? He met them at their point of pain. Though death has been destroyed and sin annulled, he has not retired. The resurrected Lord has once again wrapped himself in flesh, put on human clothes, and searched out hurting hearts.

1. There are many stories of disappointment, confusion, and sorrow in the Scriptures, and some writers bared their hearts and shared their pain.

   • How does David describe the state of his heart in Psalm 38:8?

   _____

   _____

   _____

   • What does sorrow do for the spirit, according to Proverbs 15:13?

   _____

   _____

   _____

   • In the face of heartbreak, what promise from Psalm 34:18 can we hold on to?

   _____

   _____

   _____

2. Though these two disciples didn't realize it, their Lord was right there with them. What promise from Deuteronomy 31:8 was he keeping?

   _____

   _____

   _____

We're talking heartbreak. We're talking about what two friends of Jesus were feeling a couple of days after his death. Their world has tumbled in on them. It's obvious by the way they walk. Their feet shuffle, their heads hang, their shoulders droop. The seven miles from Jerusalem to Emmaus must feel like seventy.

HE STILL MOVES STONES

3. Jesus had told them what was to come, but they didn't understand. Their own expectations got in the way. Their disappointment clouded their perspective. How did Paul describe this kind of understanding in 1 Corinthians 13:12?

_____

_____

_____

Disappointment is caused by unmet expectations. Disappointment is cured by revamped expectations. So Jesus sets about the task of restructuring their expectations. You know what he did? He told them the story. Not just any story. He told them the story of God and God's plan for people. "Then starting with what Moses and all the prophets had said about him, Jesus began to explain everything that had been written about himself in the Scriptures" (Luke 24:27 NCV).

Fascinating. Jesus' cure for the broken heart is the story of God. He started with Moses and finished with himself. Why did he do that? Why did he retell the ancient tale? Why did he go all the way back two thousand years to the story of Moses? I think I know the reason. I know because what they heard is what we all need to hear when we are disappointed.

We need to hear that God is still in control. We need to hear that it's not over until he says so. We need to hear that life's mishaps and tragedies are not a reason to bail out. They are simply a reason to sit tight.

4. What does Jesus claim to fulfill in Luke 24:44?

_____

_____

See, O LORD, that I am in distress; my soul is troubled; my heart is overturned within me.

LAMENTATIONS 1:20

5. In Acts 10:43, what does Peter say about the prophecies of the Old Testament?

_____

_____

6. What do the Messianic prophecies and the New Testament scriptures reveal about the character and ministry of Christ?

Prophecy	Revelation
Exodus 15:11	2 Corinthians 5:21
_____	_____
_____	_____
Isaiah 9:1–2	Matthew 4:12–17
_____	_____
_____	_____
Isaiah 53:12	John 10:11
_____	_____
_____	_____

7. If we are wise, what will we pay attention to, according to 2 Peter 1:19?

_____

_____

8. How did the two who were on the road to Emmaus describe the experience of being taught by the Lord, according to Luke 24:32?

_____

_____

9. John begins and ends the book of Revelation with blessings. What are they?

- Revelation 1:3

_____

_____

- Revelation 22:7

_____

_____

The way to deal with discouragement? The cure for disappointment? Go back to the story. Read it again and again. Be reminded that you aren't the first person to weep. And you aren't the first person to be helped.

Read the story and remember, their story is yours!

The challenge too great? Read the story. That's you crossing the Red Sea with Moses.

Too many worries? Read the story. That's you receiving heavenly food with the Israelites.

Your wounds too deep? Read the story. That's you, Joseph, forgiving your brothers for betraying you.

Your enemies too mighty? Read the story. That's you marching with Jehoshaphat into a battle already won.

Your disappointments too heavy? Read the story of the Emmaus-bound disciples. The Savior they thought was dead now walked beside them. He entered their house and sat at their table. And something happened in their hearts. "It felt like a fire burning in us when Jesus talked to us on the road and explained the Scriptures to us" (Luke 24:32 NCV).

Next time you're disappointed, don't panic. Don't jump out. Don't give up. Just be patient and let God remind you he's still in control. It ain't over till it's over.

Selections throughout this lesson were taken from *Just Like Jesus* and *He Still Moves Stones.*

1. Matthew 11:15; 13:9; 13:43; Mark 4:9; 4:23; 8:18; Luke 8:8; 14:35; Revelation 2:7; 2:11; 2:17; 2:29; 3:6; 3:13; 3:22; 13:9. **2.** Mark 4:1–20. **3.** Revelation 2:7; 2:11; 2:17; 2:29; 3:6; 3:13; 3:22; 13:9 (NIV).

NOTES

NOTES

He's Forgiving

DAY ONE
I am the Messiah . . .

HER EYES SQUINT against the noonday sun. Her shoulders stoop under the weight of the water jar. Her feet trudge, stirring dust on the path. She keeps her eyes down so she can dodge the stares of the others.

She is a Samaritan; she knows the sting of racism. She is a woman; she's bumped her head on the ceiling of sexism. She's been married to five men. Five. Five different marriages. Five different beds. Five different rejections. She knows the sound of slamming doors.

She knows what it means to love and receive no love in return. Her current mate won't even give her his name. He only gives her a place to sleep.

On this particular day, she came to the well at noon. Why hadn't she gone in the early morning with the other women? Maybe she had. Maybe she just needed an extra draw of water on a hot day. Or maybe not. Maybe it was the other women she was avoiding. A walk in the hot sun was a small price to pay in order to escape their sharp tongues.

The woman said to Him, "I know that Messiah is coming" (who is called Christ). "When He comes, He will tell us all things." Jesus said to her, "I who speak to you am He."
JOHN 4:25–26

"Here she comes."

"Have you heard? She's got a new man!"

"They say she'll sleep with anyone."

"Shhh. There she is."

So she came to the well at noon. She expected silence. She expected solitude. Instead, she found one who knew her better than she knew herself.

He was seated on the ground: legs outstretched, hands folded, back resting against the well. His eyes were closed. She stopped and looked at him. She looked around. No one was near. She looked back at him. He was obviously Jewish. What was he doing here? His eyes opened, and hers ducked in embarrassment. She went quickly about her task.

Sensing her discomfort, Jesus asked her for water. But she was too streetwise to think that all he wanted was a drink. "Since when does an uptown fellow like you ask a girl like me for water?" She wanted to know what he really had in mind. Her intuition was partly correct. He was interested in more than water. He was interested in her heart.

They talked. Who could remember the last time a man had spoken to her with respect?

He told her about a spring of water that would quench, not the thirst of the throat, but of the soul.

1. Whom did Jesus call "blessed" in Matthew 5:6? What does it mean? What are the promises for living this kind of life?

_____

_____

_____

_____

_____

2. Others spoke of their longing for God as thirstiness—especially
   David. In each of the following psalms, what is that longing for God
   specifically compared to?

   Psalm 42:1–2

   _____

   _____

   Psalm 63:1

   _____

   _____

   Psalm 107:9

   _____

   _____

   Psalm 143:6

   _____

   _____

   _____

3. Does God leave us wanting when we thirst after him? Of course not.
   What does he promise in Isaiah 44:3?

   _____

   _____

4. In John 4:13–15, Jesus tells the Samaritan woman of "water spring-
   ing up into everlasting life," but this isn't the only time he mentions
   living water.

   • What does Jesus teach in John 6:35?

   _____

   _____

- In John 7:37, what invitation does Jesus offer?

_____

_____

- What does the Lord promise in Revelation 21:6?

_____

_____

> And the Spirit and the bride say, "Come!" And let him who hears say, "Come!" And let him who thirsts come. Whoever desires, let him take the water of life freely.
>
> REVELATION 22:17

That intrigued her. "Sir, give me this water so that I won't get thirsty and have to keep coming here to draw water" (John 4:15 NIV).

"Go, call your husband and come back" (v. 16 NIV).

Her heart must have sunk. Here was a Jew who didn't care if she was a Samaritan. Here was a man who didn't look down on her as a woman. Here was the closest thing to gentleness she'd ever seen. And now he was asking her about . . . that.

Anything but that. Maybe she considered lying. "Oh, my husband? He's busy." Maybe she wanted to change the subject. Perhaps she wanted to leave—but she stayed. And she told the truth.

"I have no husband" (v. 17 NIV). (Kindness has a way of inviting honesty.)

You probably know the rest of the story. I wish you didn't. I wish you were hearing it for the first time. For if you were, you'd be wide-eyed as you waited to see what Jesus would do next. Why? Because you've wanted to do the same thing.

You've wanted to take off your mask. You've wanted to stop pretending. You've wondered what God would do if you opened your cobweb-covered door of secret sin.

This woman wondered what Jesus would do. She must have wondered if the kindness would cease when the truth was revealed. *He will be angry. He will leave. He will think I'm worthless.*

If you've had the same anxieties, then get out your pencil. You'll want to underline Jesus' answer.

"You're right. You have had five husbands, and the man you are with now won't even give you a name."

No criticism? No anger? No what-kind-of-mess-have-you-made-of-your-life lectures?

No. It wasn't perfection that Jesus was seeking; it was honesty.

5. What assurances can the honest find in Psalm 32:5?

_____

_____

The woman was amazed.

"I can see that you are a prophet" (v. 19 NIV). Translation? "There is something different about you. Do you mind if I ask you something?"

Then she asked the question that revealed the gaping hole in her soul.

"Where is God? My people say he is on the mountain. Your people say he is in Jerusalem. I don't know where he is."

6. Jesus tells her things only a prophet would know. What does Psalm 44:21 say the Lord knows?

_____

_____

7. If he knows this much, perhaps he can tell her more. The Samaritan woman is seeking. Her heart yearns for living water. Her soul cries out to find God. Her prayer might have echoed Psalm 139:23 at this moment. What does this verse invite God to do?

_____

_____

I'd give a thousand sunsets to see the expression on Jesus' face as he heard those words. Did his eyes water? Did he smile? Did he look up into the clouds and wink at his father?

Of all the places to find a hungry heart—Samaria?

Of all the Samaritans to be searching for God—a woman?

Of all the women to have an insatiable appetite for God—a five-time divorcée?

And of all the people to be chosen to personally receive the secret of the ages, an outcast among outcasts? The most "insignificant" person in the region?

Remarkable. Jesus didn't reveal the secret to King Herod. He didn't request an audience of the Sanhedrin and tell them the news. It wasn't within the colonnades of a Roman court that he announced his identity.

No, it was in the shade of a well in a rejected land to an ostracized woman. His eyes must have danced as he whispered the secret.

"I am the Messiah." ✳

Behold! My Servant whom I uphold, My Elect One in whom My soul delights! I have put My Spirit upon Him; He will bring forth justice to the Gentiles. He will not cry out, nor raise His voice, nor cause His voice to be heard in the street. A bruised reed He will not break, and smoking flax He will not quench; He will bring forth justice for truth.

ISAIAH 42:1–3

DAY TWO
Only one thing is
important . . .

*And Jesus answered and said
to her, "Martha, Martha,
you are worried and
troubled about many things.
But one thing is needed, and
Mary has chosen that good
part, which will not be
taken away from her."*
LUKE 10:41–42

I LOVE MILK. I am a confessed milkaholic. One of the saddest days of my life was when I learned that whole milk was unhealthy. With great reluctance I have adapted to the watered-down version—but on occasion I still allow myself the hallowed ecstasy of a cold glass of whole milk and a hot, gooey, chocolate-chip cookie.

In my years of appreciating the fine fruit of the cow, I have learned that a high price is paid for leaving milk out of the refrigerator. (On one occasion I spewed the spoiled stuff all over the kitchen cabinet.) Sweet milk turns sour from being too warm too long.

Sweet dispositions turn sour for the same reason. Let aggravation stew without a period of cooling down, and the result? A bad, bitter, clabberish attitude.

The tenth chapter of Luke describes the step-by-step process of the sweet becoming sour.

It's the story of Martha. A dear soul given to hospitality and organization. More frugal than frivolous, more practical than pensive, Martha runs her household like a tight ship, and she is a stern captain. Ask her to choose between a book and a broom, and she'll take the broom.

Mary, however, will take the book. Mary is Martha's sister. Same parents, different priorities. Martha has things to do. Mary has thoughts to think. The dishes can wait. Let Martha go to the market; Mary will go to the library.

Two sisters. Two personalities. And as long as they understand each other, it's hand in glove. But when the one resents the other, it's flint and stone.

Let's say we quietly step in the back door of Martha's kitchen, and I'll show you what I mean. (One warning: Stay away from the milk; it's beginning to sour.)

Shhh, there she is. Over by the table. The one wearing the apron. My, look at her work! I told you this lady knows how to run a kitchen. How does she do that? Stirring with one hand, cracking eggs with the other. And nothing spills. She knows what she's doing.

Must be a big crowd. There's lots of food. That's them laughing in the next room. Sounds like they're having fun.

But Martha isn't. One look at the flour-covered scowl will tell you that.

"Stupid sister."

What? Did you hear her mumble something?

"That Mary. Here I am alone in the kitchen while she's out there."

Hmm. Seems the oven isn't the only thing hot in here.

"Wouldn't have invited Jesus over if I'd known he was gonna bring the whole army. Those guys eat like horses, and that Peter always belches."

Oh boy. She's miffed. Look at her glaring over her shoulder through the doorway. That's Mary she's staring at. The one seated on the floor, listening to Jesus.

"Little sweet sister . . . always ready to listen and never ready to work. I wouldn't mind sitting down myself. But all I do is cook and sew, cook and sew. Well, enough is enough!"

Watch out! There she goes. Someone's about to get it.

"Lord, don't you care that my sister has left me alone to do all the work? Tell her to help me" (v. 40 NCV).

Suddenly the room goes silent, deathly silent except for the tap-tap-tapping of Martha's foot on the stone floor and the slapping of a wooden spoon in her palm. She looms above the others—flour on her cheeks and fire in her eyes.

We have to chuckle at the expression on the faces of the disciples. They stare wide-eyed at this fury that hell hath not known. And poor Mary, flushed red with embarrassment, sighs and sinks lower to the floor.

Only Jesus speaks. For only Jesus understands the problem. The problem is not the large crowd. The problem is not Mary's choice to listen. The problem is not Martha's choice to host. The problem is Martha's heart, a heart soured with anxiety.

"Martha, Martha, you are worried and upset about many things" (v. 41 NCV). Bless her heart, Martha wanted to do right. But bless her heart, her heart was wrong.

1. It's impossible to hide what's in our heart from the Lord. He knows us far too well. Take a look at the following verses, and match them with the truth they teach.

    ___ 1 Samuel 16:7   a. God searches out the secrets of the heart.

    ___ 2 Chronicles 6:30   b. God knows our hearts and our souls.

    ___ Psalm 44:21   c. God weighs, or examines, our hearts.

    ___ Psalm 139:2   d. God does not see as man sees.

    ___ Proverbs 21:2   e. God tests the mind.

    ___ Proverbs 24:12   f. God alone knows the hearts of men.

    ___ Jeremiah 12:3   g. The Lord of Hosts, the Lord Almighty, tests or examines the righteous.

    ___ Jeremiah 17:10   h. God understands our thoughts.

    ___ Jeremiah 20:12   i. You, O Lord, know me!

2. Fretting is just another name for worrying. What does Psalm 37:8 say is the result of a heart that worries? How does worry affect you?

    _____

    _____

    _____

Apparently Martha worried too much, too. So much so that she started bossing God around. Worry will do that to you. It makes you forget who's in charge.

What makes this case interesting, however, is that Martha worried about something good. She was having Jesus over for dinner. She was literally serving God. Her aim was to please Jesus. But she made a common, yet dangerous mistake. As she began to work for him, her work became more important than her Lord. What began as a way to serve Jesus, slowly and subtly became a way to serve self.

Slaves, obey your earthly masters with deep respect and fear. Serve them sincerely as you would serve Christ. Try to please them at all times, not just when they are watching you. As slaves of Christ, do the will of God with all your heart. Work with enthusiasm, as though you were working for the Lord rather than for people.

EPHESIANS 6:5–7 NLT

3. When it comes to a servant's heart, Jesus sets the example. We are told that he "did not come to be served, but to serve" (Matthew 20:28). Consider the following statements about our service to the Lord. Are they true or false?

____ God notices our good works, even if no one else seems to (Revelation 2:19).

____ God takes anything he can get—half-hearted service is better than nothing (Revelation 3:15–16).

____ In service, it's the final product that counts, not our attitude (Psalm 100:2).

____ One way to serve the Lord is to serve one another (Galatians 5:13–14).

____ You can't serve two masters, whether it's God and money . . . or God and self (Matthew 6:24).

____ It's often tempting to make a show of serving in the hopes of gaining admiration (Ephesians 6:5–7).

4. Martha fell into the trap of thinking that her efforts deserved recognition. Her heart was wrong, and God knew it. When we serve him, what sort of attitude does he want to find? What does 1 Chronicles 29:17 say?

_____

_____

5. What guideline for conduct do we find in Philippians 1:27? Especially, how does Paul say we should act in our relationship to fellow believers?

_____

_____

6. What would have pleased God more than a perfectly turned-out dinner, according to Psalm 51:17?

_____

_____

There is a principle here. To keep an attitude from souring, treat it like you would a cup of milk. Cool it off.

Martha's life was cluttered. She needed a break. "Martha, Martha, you are worried and upset about many things," the Master explained to her. "Only one thing is important. Mary has chosen [it]" (Luke 10:41–42 NCV).

What had Mary chosen? She had chosen to sit at the feet of Christ. God is more pleased with the quiet attention of a sincere servant than the noisy service of a sour one.

By the way, this story could easily have been reversed. Mary could have been the one to get angry. The sister on the floor could have resented the sister at the sink. Mary could have grabbed Jesus and dragged him into the kitchen and said, "Tell Martha to quit being so productive and to get reflective. Why do I have to do all the thinking and praying around here?"

What matters more than the type of service is the heart behind the service. A bad attitude spoils the gift we leave on the altar for God. ✳

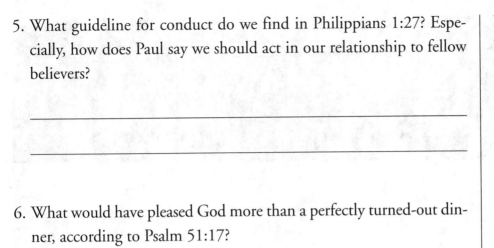

It's easy to forget who is the servant and who is to be served.
HE STILL MOVES STONES

A rebel shouts in anger; a wise man holds his temper in and cools it.
PROVERBS 29:11 TLB

The sacrifices of God are a broken spirit, a broken and a contrite heart; these, O God, You will not despise.
PSALM 51:17

*A certain man had two
sons. . . . the younger
son gathered all together,
journeyed to a far country,
and there wasted his
possessions with
prodigal living.*
LUKE 15:11, 13

THE CASE of the elder brother.

A difficult one because he looked so good. He kept his room straight and his nose clean. He played by the rules and paid all his dues. His résumé? Impeccable. His credit? Squeaky clean. And loyalty? While his brother was sowing wild oats, he stayed home and sowed the crops.

On the outside he was everything a father could want in a son. But on the inside he was sour and hollow. Overcome by jealousy. Consumed by anger. Blinded by bitterness.

You remember the story. It's perhaps the best known of all the parables Jesus told.

Then there is the lost son. The boy who broke his father's heart by taking his inheritance and taking off. He trades his dignity for a whisky bottle and his self-respect for a pigpen. Then comes the son's sorrow and his decision to go home. He hopes his dad will give him a job on the farm and an apartment over the garage. What he finds is a father who has kept his absent son's place set at the table and the porch light on every night.

The father is so excited to see his son, you'll never guess what he does. That's right! He throws a party! We party-loving prodigals love what he did, but it infuriated the elder brother.

"The older son was angry" (Luke 15:28 NCV). It's not hard to see why. "So, is this how a guy gets recognition in this family? Get drunk and go broke, and you get a party?" So he sat outside the house and pouted.

1. Anger isn't the best place to hole up when things aren't going your way. In fact, the Bible says we're wise to avoid angry people.

   • What's Solomon's assessment of angry women in Proverbs 21:19?

   _____

   _____

   • The angry man isn't any better. How does Proverbs 22:24 tell us to deal with him?

   _____

   _____

   • According to Proverbs 29:22, what is the result of a life ruled by one's temper?

   _____

   _____

2. Anger can flare up in an instant, or it can simmer long and low. Either way, it's a problem that must be addressed. Match these words of wisdom with the verse in which they're found.

   ___ Psalm 4:4   a. Those who harbor anger in their hearts are fools.

   ___ Ecclesiastes 7:9   b. God is able to turn away from his anger and forgive.

   ___ Isaiah 12:1   c. Don't let the sun go down on your wrath.

   ___ Matthew 5:22   d. Refrain from anger, malice, and profanity.

   ___ Ephesians 4:26   e. When you're angry, do not sin.

   ___ Colossians 3:8   f. Angry words are a sin worthy of condemnation.

3. What does Paul say to do with our bitterness, anger, and wrath, according to Ephesians 4:31?

_____

_____

The older brother felt he was a victim of inequity. When his father came out to find him, the son started at the top, listing the atrocities of his life. To hear him say it, his woes began the day he was born.

> "I have served you like a slave for many years and have always obeyed your commands. But you never gave me even a young goat to have at a feast with my friends. But your other son, who wasted all your money on prostitutes, comes home, and you kill the fat calf for him!" (Luke 15:29–30 NCV).

> Appears that both sons spent time in the pigpen. One in the pen of rebellion—the other in the pen of self-pity. The younger one has come home. The older one hasn't. He's still in the slop. He is saying the same thing you said when the kid down the street got a bicycle and you didn't. It's not fair!

> Victims grumble. They're angry at others who got what they didn't.

> They sulk. The world is against them.

> They accuse. The pictures of their enemies are darted to the wall.

> They boast. "I followed the rules. I played fairly . . . in fact, better than anybody else."

> They whine. "Nobody listens to me. Nobody remembers me. Nobody cares about me."

4. "It's not fair!" Read the parable of the vineyard workers in Matthew 20:1–16, and answer the following questions.

- What agreement did the landowner make with the laborers in verse 2?

  _____

  _____

- Did he stick to his word?

  _____

  _____

- What happened to the expectations of those first workmen between verses 8 and 10?

  _____

  _____

- How would you feel if you were one of those early laborers?

  _____

  _____

- How would you feel if you had been one of the "eleventh hour" laborers?

  _____

  _____

- Was the landowner unfair?

  _____

  _____

You can choose, like many, to chain yourself to your hurt.

Or you can choose, like some, to put away your hurts before they become hates. You can choose to go to the party.

You have a place there. Your name is beside a plate. If you are a child of God, no one can take away your sonship.

Which is precisely what the father said to the older son. "Son, you are always with me, and all that I have is yours" (Luke 15:31 NCV).

And that is precisely what the Father says to you. How does God deal with your bitter heart? He reminds you that what you have is more important than what you don't have.

The Spirit Himself bears witness with our spirit that we are children of God, and if children, then heirs—heirs of God and joint heirs with Christ.

ROMANS 8:16–17

5. What are we to God, according to Galatians 4:7?

_____

_____

6. We are heirs, and an heir receives an inheritance. What does being a child of God entitle us to? Shall we make a list?

Romans 11:33 _____

Ephesians 1:7 _____

Ephesians 3:8 _____

Ephesians 3:16 _____

Philippians 4:19 _____

Colossians 2:2 _____

7. Are these earthly riches? No, nothing so uncertain. The wealth of this world is transient.

• What does James 2:5 say to those who are poor?

_____

_____

- What does 1 Timothy 6:17 have to say to those who are rich?

_____

_____

8. What do we have to look forward to, according to Ephesians 2:6–7?

_____

_____

You still have your relationship with God. No one can take that. No one can touch it.

Your health can be taken and your money stolen—but your place at God's table is permanent.

The brother was bitter because he focused on what he didn't have and forgot what he did have. His father reminded him—and us—that he had everything he'd always had.

Wise are we to follow the father's advice. Wise are we if we rise above our hurts. For if we do, we'll be present at the Father's final celebration. A party to end all parties. A party where no pouters will be permitted.

Why don't you come and join the fun? ✳

Go and sin
no more . . .

*Now early in the
morning He came again
into the temple, and all
the people came to Him;
and He sat down and
taught them. Then the
scribes and Pharisees
brought to Him a
woman caught
in adultery.*
JOHN 8:2–3

THIS WOMAN'S STORY is a story of failure. A story of abuse. A story of shame. And a story of grace.

That's her, the woman standing in the center of the circle. Those men around her are religious leaders. Pharisees, they are called. Self-appointed custodians of conduct. And the other man, the one in the simple clothes, the one sitting on the ground, the one looking at the face of the woman, that's Jesus.

Jesus has been teaching.

The woman has been cheating.

And the Pharisees are out to stop them both.

"Teacher, this woman was caught in the act of adultery" (John 8:4 NIV). The accusation rings off the courtyard walls.

"Caught in the act of adultery." The words alone are enough to make you blush. Doors slammed open. Covers jerked back.

"In the act." In the arms. In the moment. In the embrace.

"Caught." Aha! What have we here? This man is not your husband. Put on some clothes! We know what to do with women like you!

In an instant she is yanked from private passion to public spectacle. Heads poke out of windows as the posse pushes her through the streets. Dogs bark. Neighbors turn. The city sees. Clutching a thin robe around her shoulders, she hides her nakedness.

But nothing can hide her shame.

From this second on, she'll be known as an adulteress. When she goes to the market, women will whisper. When she passes, heads will turn. When her name is mentioned, the people will remember.

Moral failure finds easy recall.

The woman stares at the ground. Her sweaty hair dangles. Her tears drip hot with hurt. Her lips are tight; her jaw is clenched. She knows she's been framed. No need to look up. She'll find no kindness. She looks at the stones in their hands. Squeezed so tightly that fingertips turn white.

She thinks of running. But where? She could claim mistreatment. But to whom? She could deny the act, but she was seen. She could beg for mercy, but these men offer none.

The woman has nowhere to turn.

1. The words of Ezra 9:6 are appropriate here. What confession is made to God in this verse?

_____

_____

2. Those who laid their trap may have seemed holy. Their righteous indignation was impressive. Yet what reminder does 1 Timothy 5:24 give?

_____

_____

3. Can any of us claim to be without sin?

   • What was Solomon's assessment in Ecclesiastes 7:20?

   _____

   _____

- Who does Romans 3:19 say is guilty?

_____

_____

- According to Galatians 3:22, who has sinned?

_____

_____

> He who covers his sins will not prosper, but whoever confesses and forsakes them will have mercy.
>
> PROVERBS 28:13

4. At the very least, we can claim to be better than the next fellow . . . right? Think again. What eye-opening truth do we find in James 2:10?

_____

_____

What does Jesus do? (If you already know, pretend you don't and feel the surprise.)

Jesus writes in the sand.

He stoops down and draws in the dirt. The same finger that engraved the commandments on Sinai's peak and seared the warning on Belshazzar's wall now scribbles in the court-yard floor. And as he writes, he speaks: "Anyone here who has never sinned can throw the first stone at her" (John 8:7 NCV).

5. These scribes and Pharisees were known for their righteousness, but this statement gave them pause. What was Jesus' opinion of their up-right behavior, according to Matthew 5:20?

_____

_____

6. What does 1 John 1:10 say about our claims to righteousness?

_____

_____

7. In the end only One could have condemned her. How is he described in these verses?

2 Corinthians 5:21 _____

Hebrews 7:26 _____

1 John 3:5_____

To the Lord our God belong mercy and forgiveness, though we have rebelled against Him.

DANIEL 9:9

The young look to the old. The old look in their hearts. They are the first to drop their stones. And as they turn to leave, the young who were cocky with borrowed convictions do the same. The only sound is the thud of rocks and the shuffle of feet.

Jesus and the woman are left alone. With the jury gone, the courtroom becomes the judge's chambers, and the woman awaits his verdict. *Surely, a sermon is brewing. No doubt, he's going to demand that I apologize.* But the judge doesn't speak. His head is down; perhaps he's still writing in the sand. He seems surprised when he realizes that she is still there.

"Woman, where are they? Has no one judged you guilty?"

She answers, "No one, sir."

Then Jesus says, "I also don't judge you guilty. You may go now, but don't sin anymore" (John 8:10–11 NCV).

If you have ever wondered how God reacts when you fail, frame these words and hang them on the wall. Read them. Ponder them. Drink from them. Stand below them and let them wash over your soul.

Let him stand beside you as you retell the events of the darkest nights of your soul.

And then listen. Listen carefully. He's speaking.

"I don't judge you guilty."

8. Rather than condemn her, Jesus told the woman to go on her way: "Go and sin no more" (John 8:11). How does Paul phrase it in 1 Corinthians 15:34?

_____

_____

9. Jesus set us free from the power of sin. Since we are no longer slaves to sin, we are urged to pursue righteousness instead.

___ Psalm 34:14   a. We are no longer instruments of unrighteousness.

___ Romans 6:2   b. Turn from evil and do good.

___ Romans 6:13   c. Flee youthful lusts, pursuing righteousness instead.

___ Romans 6:18   d. Cease from sin.

___ 2 Timothy 2:22   e. We have died to sin, so why live in it?

___ 1 Peter 4:1   f. We are free from sin and slaves to righteousness.

NICODEMUS CAME in the middle of the night. The centurion came in the middle of the day. The leper and the sinful woman appeared in the middle of crowds. Zacchaeus appeared in the middle of a tree. Matthew had a party for him.

The educated. The powerful. The rejected. The sick. The lonely. The wealthy. Who would have ever assembled such a crew? All they had in common were their empty hope chests, long left vacant by charlatans and profiteers. Though they had nothing to offer, they asked for everything: a new birth, a second chance, a fresh start, a clean conscience. And without exception their requests were honored.

And now, one more beggar comes with a request. Only minutes from the death of them both, he stands before the King. He will ask for crumbs. And he, like the others, will receive a whole loaf.

Skull's hill—windswept and stony. The thief—gaunt and pale.

Hinges squeak as the door of death closes on his life.

His situation is pitiful. He's taking the last step down the spiral staircase of failure. One crime after another. One rejection after another. Lower and lower he descended until he reached the bottom—a crossbeam and three spikes.

He can't hide who he is. His only clothing is the cloak of his disgrace. No fancy jargon. No impressive résumé. No Sunday school awards. Just a naked history of failure.

He sees Jesus.

Assuredly, I say to you, today you will be with Me in Paradise.
LUKE 23:43

Earlier he had mocked the man. When the crowd first chorused its criticism, he'd sung his part (Matthew 27:44). But now he doesn't mock Jesus. He studies him. He begins to wonder who this man might be.

How strange. He doesn't resist the nails; he almost invites them.

He hears the jests and the insults and sees the man remain quiet. He sees the fresh blood on Jesus' cheeks, the crown of thorns scraping Jesus' scalp, and he hears the hoarse whisper, "Father, forgive them."

Why do they want him dead?

Slowly the thief's curiosity offsets the pain in his body. He momentarily forgets the nails rubbing against the raw bones of his wrists and the cramps in his calves.

He begins to feel a peculiar warmth in his heart: he begins to care; he begins to care about this peaceful martyr.

There's no anger in his eyes, only tears.

He looks at the huddle of soldiers throwing dice in the dirt, gambling for a ragged robe. He sees the sign above Jesus' head. It's painted with sarcasm: King of the Jews.

They mock him as a king. If he were crazy, they would ignore him. If he had no followers, they'd turn him away. If he were nothing to fear, they wouldn't kill him. You only kill a king if he has a kingdom.

Could it be . . .

His cracked lips open to speak.

Then, all of a sudden, his thoughts are exploded by the accusations of the criminal on the other cross. He, too, has been studying Jesus, but studying through the blurred lens of cynicism.

"So you're the Messiah, are you? Prove it by saving yourself—and us, too, while you're at it!" (Luke 23:39 TLB).

It's an inexplicable dilemma—how two people can hear the same words and see the same Savior, and one see hope and the other see nothing but himself.

It was all the first criminal could take. Perhaps the crook who hurled the barb expected the other crook to take the cue and hurl a few of his own. But he didn't. No second verse was sung. What the bitter-tongued criminal did hear were words of defense.

"Don't you fear God?"

Only minutes before, these same lips had cursed Jesus. Now they are defending him. Every head on the hill lifts to look at this one who spoke on behalf of the Christ. Every angel weeps and every demon gapes.

Who could have imagined this thief thinking of anyone but himself? He'd always been the bully, the purse-snatching brat. Who could remember the last time he'd come to someone's aid? But as the last grains of sand trickle through his hourglass, he performs man's noblest act. He speaks on God's behalf.

1. In the last hours of his life, this man's eyes were opened, and he saw Jesus for who he really was. How does Acts 26:18 describe this turning?

_____

_____

2. The thief speaks up. What does Matthew 10:32 say about those who confess their belief before others?

_____

_____

3. He had broken the Law, but that didn't matter with the Lord. What does John 1:17 say became available through Jesus?

_____

_____

4. To satisfy sin's great debt, a sacrifice was required. Why did Jesus come to earth in the first place, according to Matthew 20:28?

_____

_____

Where are those we would expect to defend Jesus?

> A much more spiritual Peter has abandoned him.

> A much more educated Pilate has washed his hands of him.

> A much more loyal mob of countrymen has demanded his death.

> A much more faithful band of disciples has scattered.

> When it seems that everyone has turned away, a crook places himself between Jesus and the accusers and speaks on his behalf.

> "Don't you even fear God when you are dying? We deserve to die for our evil deeds, but this man hasn't done one thing wrong" (Luke 23:40–41 TLB).

5. Jesus was a sinless sacrifice. The thief was right; Jesus had done nothing wrong.

- What was required for eternal redemption, according to Hebrews 9:12?

_____

_____

- In 1 Peter 1:19, what is Jesus called?

_____

_____

- How does Paul describe Jesus' sacrifice in Galatians 3:13?

_____

_____

6. There, in the very presence of the blood that was being shed for him, the thief on the cross glimpsed grace. Write out these verses in the space provided:

Romans 5:15

_____

_____

Ephesians 1:7

_____

_____

7. God gives grace to the humble (Proverbs 3:34), and this sinner found grace. What made it possible for him to join Jesus in heaven, according to Revelation 1:5?

_____

_____

The soldiers look up. The priests cease chattering. Mary wipes her tears and raises her eyes. No one had even noticed the fellow, but now everyone looks at him.

Perhaps even Jesus looks at him. Perhaps he turns to see the one who had spoken when all others had remained silent. Perhaps he fights to focus his eyes on the one who offered this final gesture of love he'd receive while alive. I wonder, did he smile as this sheep straggled into the fold?

For that, in effect, is exactly what the criminal is doing. He is stumbling to safety just as the gate is closing. Lodged in the thief's statement are the two facts that anyone needs to recognize in order to come to Jesus. Look at the phrase again. Do you see them?

"We are getting what we deserve. This man has done nothing wrong."

We are guilty and he is innocent.

We are filthy and he is pure.

We are wrong and he is right.

He is not on that cross for his sins. He is there for ours.

And once the crook understands this, his request seems only natural. As he looks into the eyes of his last hope, he makes the same request any Christian has made.

"Remember me when you come into your kingdom" (Luke 23:42 NIV).

No stained-glass homilies. No excuses. Just a desperate plea for help.

At this point Jesus performs the greatest miracle of the cross. Greater than the earthquake. Greater than the tearing of the temple curtain. Greater than the darkness. Greater than the resurrected saints appearing on the streets.

He performs the miracle of forgiveness. A sin-soaked criminal is received by a blood-stained Savior.

"Today you will be with me in Paradise. This is a solemn promise" (v. 43 TLB).

Wow. Only seconds before, the thief was a beggar nervously squeezing his hat at the castle door, wondering if the King might spare a few crumbs. Suddenly he's holding the whole pantry.

Such is the definition of grace.

Selections throughout this lesson taken from *Six Hours One Friday* and *He Still Moves Stones*.

NOTES

He's Still Speaking

YOU ARE TIRED.

You are weary.

Weary of being slapped by the waves of broken dreams.

Weary of being stepped on and run over in the endless marathon to the top.

Weary of trusting in someone only to have that trust returned in an envelope with no return address.

Weary of staring into the future and seeing only futility.

Few things can weary you more than the fast pace of the human race. Too many sprints for success. Too many laps in the gray-flannel fast lane. Too many nine-to-five masquerade parties. Too many days of doing whatever it takes eventually take their toll. You are left gasping for air, holding your sides on the side of the track.

And it isn't the late night reports or countless airports that sap your strength as much as it is the question you dare

Come to Me, all you who labor and are heavy laden, and I will give you rest. Take My yoke upon you and learn from Me, for I am gentle and lowly in heart, and you will find rest for your souls. For My yoke is easy and My burden is light.
MATTHEW 11:28–30

not admit you are asking yourself. *Is it worth it? When I get what I want, will it be worth the price I paid?*

1. David knew what it was like to be weighed down. What does he say in Psalm 38:4?

_____

_____

2. What longing is expressed in Psalm 55:6?

_____

_____

Futility, failure, and finality. The three Fs on the human report card. The three burdens that are too big for any back, too heavy for any biceps. Three burdens that no man can carry alone.

SIX HOURS ONE FRIDAY

The result? A person slugging his way through life, weighed down by the past. I don't know if you've noticed, but it's hard to be thoughtful when you're carrying your burdens. It's hard to be affirming when you are affirmation-starved. It's hard to be forgiving when you feel guilty.

Paul had an interesting observation about the way we treat people. He said it about marriage, but the principle applies in any relationship. "The man who loves his wife loves himself" (Ephesians 5:28 NCV). There is a correlation between the way you feel about yourself and the way you feel about others. If you are at peace with yourself—if you like yourself—you will get along with others.

The converse is also true. If you don't like yourself—if you are ashamed, embarrassed, or angry—other people are going to know it. The tragedy is that we tend to throw our stones at those we love.

Unless the cycle is interrupted.

Which takes us to the question, "How *does* a person get relief?"

3. There's no need to continue in our weariness. What are we invited to do in Psalm 55:22?

_____

_____

Come aside by yourselves to a deserted place and rest a while.

MARK 6:31

I can see you holding this book and shaking your head. "I've read the Bible, I've sat on the pew—but I've never received relief."

If that is the case, could I ask a delicate but deliberate question? Could it be that you went to religion and didn't go to God? Could it be that you went to a church but never saw Christ?

"Come to me," the verse reads.

"Come to me, all you who are weary and burdened, and I will give you rest" (Matthew 11:28 NIV).

4. What does Hebrews 12:1 encourage us to do?

_____

_____

5. When we lighten our load, we lighten our hearts.

- What does Jeremiah 6:16 say?

_____

_____

Rest in the LORD, and wait patiently for Him; do not fret.

PSALM 37:7

- In Psalm 116:7, what note of praise do we find concerning rest?

_____

_____

6. Paul says that when compared to the full weight of glory, the afflictions of this world will seem light indeed (2 Corinthians 4:17). So for now, what can we rest in, according to Acts 2:25–26?

_____

_____

7. What else do we have relief or rest from, according to Isaiah 14:3?

_____

_____

8. What is the call of Hebrews 4:11?

_____

_____

Come to me . . . The invitation is to come to him. Why him?

He offers the invitation as a penniless rabbi in an oppressed nation. He has no political office, no connections with the authorities in Rome. He hasn't written a best seller or earned a diploma.

Yet, he dares to look into the leathery faces of farmers and tired faces of housewives and offer rest. He looks into the disillusioned eyes of a preacher or two from Jerusalem. He gazes into the cynical stare of a banker and the hungry eyes of a bartender and makes this paradoxical promise: "Take my yoke upon you and learn from me, for I am gentle and humble in heart, and you will find rest for your souls" (Matthew 11:29 NIV).

The people came. They came out of the cul-de-sacs and office complexes of their day. They brought him the burdens of their existence, and he gave them not religion, not doctrine, not systems, but rest.

As a result, they called him Lord.

As a result, they called him Savior. ✳

*I*T'S A WONDERFUL DAY INDEED when we stop working for God and begin working with God. (Go ahead, read the sentence again.)

For years I viewed God as a compassionate CEO and my role as a loyal sales representative. He had his office, and I had my territory. I could contact him as much as I wanted. He was always a phone or fax away. He encouraged me, rallied behind me, and supported me, but he didn't go with me. At least I didn't think he did. Then I read 2 Corinthians 6:1: We are "God's fellow workers" (NIV).

Fellow workers? Colaborers? God and I work together? Imagine the paradigm shift this truth creates. Rather than report to God, we work *with* God. Rather than check in with him and then leave, we check in with him and then follow. We are always in the presence of God. We never leave church. There is never a nonsacred moment! His presence never diminishes. Our awareness of his presence may falter, but the reality of his presence never changes.

This leads me to a great question. If God is perpetually present, is it possible to enjoy unceasing communion with him? Would it be possible to live—*minute by minute*—in the presence of God? Is such intimacy even possible?

> *I am the vine, you are the branches. He who abides in Me, and I in him, bears much fruit.*
> JOHN 15:5

1. Paul obviously thought in terms of continuous communication with the Lord. Look at these verses, and write down what each says about praying.

   Romans 12:12 _____

   Ephesians 6:18 _____

Philippians 4:6 _____

Colossians 4:2 _____

1 Thessalonians 5:17 _____

2. The call is to abide—dwell together, remain together. David often spoke of abiding with God. What does Psalm 91:1 declare?

_____

_____

3. In John 8:31, what does Jesus say is one of the hallmarks of his disciples?

_____

_____

The truth . . . abides in us and will be with us forever.

2 JOHN 1:2

4. John frequently speaks of abiding, both in his gospel and in his letters. One of the things this disciple urges is abiding in God's Word. What does he urge believers to continue in, according to 2 John 1:9?

_____

_____

5. Jesus uses the picture of a vine and its branches to illustrate just how dependent we are on the Lord for our lives. What does he command in John 15:4, and what is the consequence if we do not obey?

_____

6. Without Jesus, what can we do, according to John 15:5? With Jesus, what can we do, according to John 15:7?

_____

_____

God wants to be as close to us as a branch is to a vine. One is an extension of the other. It's impossible to tell where one starts and the other ends. The branch isn't connected only at the moment of bearing fruit. The gardener doesn't keep the branches in a box and then, on the day he wants grapes, glue them to the vine. No, the branch constantly draws nutrition from the vine. Separation means certain death.

God also uses the temple to depict the intimacy he desires. "Don't you know," Paul writes, "that your body is the temple of the Holy Spirit, who lives in you and who was given to you by God?" (1 Corinthians 6:19 TEV). Think with me about the temple for a moment. Was God a visitor or a resident in Solomon's temple? Would you describe his presence as occasional or permanent? You know the answer. God didn't come and go, appear and disappear. He was a permanent presence, always available.

What incredibly good news for us! We are NEVER away from God! He is NEVER away from us—not even for a moment! God doesn't come to us on Sunday mornings and then exit on Sunday afternoons. He remains within us, continually present in our lives.

> God is as near to you as the vine is to the branch, as present within you as God was in the temple, as intimate with you as a husband with a wife, and as devoted to you as a shepherd to his sheep.
> JUST LIKE JESUS

7. One consequence of abiding is fruitfulness. What is Jesus' teaching in Matthew 7:17–18?

_____

_____

8. List the spiritual fruit found in Ephesians 5:9 and Galatians 5:22–23. To what extent can we produce these things ourselves?

_____

_____

_____

9. What are we called to do in 1 John 2:28?

_____

_____

People who live long lives together eventually begin to sound alike, to talk alike, even to think alike. As we walk with God, we take on his thoughts, his principles, his attitudes. We take on his heart.

Does unceasing communion seem daunting, complicated? Are you thinking, *Life is difficult enough. Why add this?* If so, remind yourself that God is the burden-remover, not the burden-giver. God intends that unceasing prayer lighten—not heighten—our load.

The more we search the Bible, the more we realize that unbroken communion with God is the intent and not the exception. Within the reach of *every* Christian is the unending presence of God. ✳

I'm an open book to you; even from a distance, you know what I'm thinking. You know when I leave and when I get back; I'm never out of your sight. You know everything I'm going to say before I start the first sentence. I look behind me and you're there, then up ahead and you're there, too—your reassuring presence, coming and going. This is too much, too wonderful—I can't take it all in!

PSALM 139:2–6 MSG

OF ALL THE TIMES we see the bowing knees of Jesus, none is so precious as when he kneels before his disciples and washes their feet.

> It was just before the Passover Feast. Jesus knew that the time had come for him to leave this world and go to the Father. Having loved his own who were in the world, he now showed them the full extent of his love.

> The evening meal was being served, and the devil had already prompted Judas Iscariot, son of Simon, to betray Jesus. Jesus knew that the Father had put all things under his power, and that he had come from God and was returning to God; so he got up from the meal, took off his outer clothing . . . and began to wash his disciples' feet, drying them with the towel that was wrapped around him (John 13:2–5 NIV).

It has been a long day. Jerusalem is packed with Passover guests, most of whom clamor for a glimpse of the Teacher. The spring sun is warm. The streets are dry. And the disciples are a long way from home. A splash of cool water would be refreshing.

The disciples enter, one by one, and take their places around the table. On the wall hangs a towel, and on the floor sits a pitcher and a basin. Any one of the disciples could volunteer for the job, but not one does.

After a few moments, Jesus stands and removes his outer garment. He wraps a servant's girdle around his waist, takes up the basin, and kneels before one of the disciples. He unlaces a sandal and gently lifts the foot and places it in the basin, covers it with water, and begins to bathe it. One by

What I am doing you do not understand now, but you will know after this.
JOHN 13:7

one, one grimy foot after another, Jesus works his way down the row.

In Jesus' day the washing of feet was a task reserved not just for servants but for the lowest of servants. Every circle has its pecking order, and the circle of household workers was no exception. The servant at the bottom of the totem pole was expected to be the one on his knees with the towel and basin.

In this case the one with the towel and basin is the king of the universe. Hands that shaped the stars now wash away filth. Fingers that formed mountains now massage toes. And the one before whom all nations will one day kneel now kneels before his disciples. Hours before his own death, Jesus' concern is singular. He wants his disciples to know how much he loves them. More than removing dirt, Jesus is removing doubt.

Jesus knows what will happen to his hands at the crucifixion. Within twenty-four hours they will be pierced and lifeless. Of all the times we'd expect him to ask for the disciples' attention, this would be one. But he doesn't.

You can be sure Jesus knows the future of these feet he is washing. These twenty-four feet will not spend the next day following their master, defending his cause. These feet will dash for cover at the flash of a Roman sword. Only one pair of feet won't abandon him in the garden. One disciple won't desert him at Gethsemane—Judas won't even make it that far! He will abandon Jesus that very night at the table.

I looked for a Bible translation that reads, "Jesus washed all the disciples' feet except the feet of Judas," but I couldn't find one. What a passionate moment when Jesus silently lifts the feet of his betrayer and washes them in the basin! Within hours the feet of Judas, cleansed by the kindness of the one he will betray, will stand in Caiaphas's court.

Behold the gift Jesus gives his followers! He knows what these men are about to do. He knows they are about to perform the vilest act of their lives. By morning they will bury their heads in shame and look down at their feet in disgust. And when they do, he wants them to remember how his knees knelt before them and he washed their feet. He wants them to realize those feet are still clean. "You don't understand now what I am doing, but you will understand later" (John 13:7 NCV).

Remarkable. He forgave their sin before they even committed it. He offered mercy before they even sought it.

1. In Psalm 51:1, we find a prayer that all our hearts can echo. What did David ask God to do for him?

_____

_____

2. Those who belong to God are called to do as he does, which means that we, too, are to be forgiving. What does Colossians 3:13 tell us to do, and why?

_____

_____

3. One reason we forgive is that we have been forgiven, but it's difficult not to want to put a limit on grace. Where did Peter want to draw the line, according to Matthew 18:21–22? How did Jesus answer?

_____

_____

4. We are urged to extend grace to those around us. What do the following verses tell us about giving grace to one another?

Colossians 4:6

_____

_____

_____

_____

5. As believers, we are called to show one another the same mercy, patience, and kindness that Jesus extended. In fact, John 13:35 says, "By this all will know that you are My disciples, if you have love for one another."

- What does Psalm 133:1 say is good and pleasant?

  _____

  _____

- How does Paul direct us in 1 Thessalonians 5:11?

  _____

  _____

- According to Ephesians 4:32, what attitude must we take toward our brothers and sisters in the Lord?

  _____

  _____

But I'm not Jesus, you object. *I could never extend grace as he did. The hurt is so deep. The wounds are so numerous. Just seeing the person causes me to cringe.* Perhaps that is your problem. Perhaps you are seeing the wrong person or at least too much of the wrong person. Remember, the secret of being just like Jesus is "fixing our eyes" on him. Try shifting your glance away from the one who hurt you and setting your eyes on the one who has saved you.

Note the promise of John, "But if we live in the light, as God is in the light, we can share fellowship with each other. Then the blood of Jesus, God's Son, cleanses us from every sin" (1 John 1:7 NCV).

"If I, your Lord and Teacher, have washed your feet, you

also should wash each other's feet. I did this as an example so that you should do as I have done for you" (John 13:14–15 NCV).

Jesus washes our feet for two reasons. The first is to give us mercy; the second is to give us a message, and that message is simply this: Jesus offers unconditional grace; we are to offer unconditional grace. The mercy of Christ preceded our mistakes; our mercy must precede the mistakes of others. Those in the circle of Christ had no doubt of his love; those in our circles should have no doubts about ours.

6. Our lives are interconnected with those around us, and we are repeatedly called to live lives characterized by a love for the brethren.

- What difficult thing does Romans 12:10 ask us to do?

   _____

   _____

- How do we learn to be loving, according to 1 Thessalonians 4:9?

   _____

   _____

- According to Hebrews 13:1, how long do we have to keep it up?

   _____

   _____

7. Describe a time or situation in which you served someone you didn't particularly like. How did that go? What was the response? How did that make you feel?

_____

_____

_____

_____

_____

YOU KNOW HOW YOU CAN READ a story you think you know and then you read it again and see something you've never seen?

You know how you can read about the same event 100 times and then on the 101st hear something so striking and new that it makes you wonder if you slept through the other times?

Maybe it's because you started in the middle of the story instead of at the beginning. Or perhaps it's because someone else reads it aloud and pauses at a place where you normally wouldn't, and POW! It hits you.

You grab the book and look at it, knowing that someone copied or read something wrong. But then you read it and well-how-do-you-do. Look at that!

Well, it happened to me. Today.

Only God knows how many times I've read the resurrection story. At least a couple of dozen Easters and a couple of hundred times in between. I've taught it. I've written about it. I've meditated on it. I've underlined it. But what I saw today I'd never seen before.

What did I see? Before I tell you, let me recount the story.

It's early dawn on Sunday morning, and the sky is dark. Those, in fact, are John's words. "It was still dark . . ." (John 20:1 NCV).

It's a dark Sunday morning. It had been dark since Friday.

Dark with Peter's denial.

Dark with the disciples' betrayal.

Do not be afraid, for I know that you seek Jesus who was crucified. He is not here; for He is risen, as He said.
MATTHEW 28:5–6

Dark with Pilate's cowardice.

Dark with Christ's anguish.

Dark with Satan's glee.

The only ember of light is the small band of women standing at a distance from the cross—watching (Matthew 27:55).

Among them are two Marys, one the mother of James and Joseph, and the other is Mary Magdalene. Why are they there? They are there to call his name. To be the final voices he hears before his death. To prepare his body for burial. They are there to clean the blood from his beard. To wipe the crimson from his legs. To close his eyes. To touch his face.

They are there. The last to leave Calvary and the first to arrive at the grave.

So early on that Sunday morning, they leave their pallets and walk out onto the tree-shadowed path. Theirs is a somber task. The morning promises only one encounter, an encounter with a corpse.

Remember, Mary and Mary don't know this is the first Easter. They are not hoping the tomb will be vacant. They aren't discussing what their response will be when they see Jesus. They have absolutely no idea that the grave has been vacated.

There was a time when they dared to dream such dreams. Not now. It's too late for the incredible. The feet that walked on water had been pierced. The hands that healed lepers had been stilled. Noble aspirations had been spiked into Friday's cross. Mary and Mary have come to place warm oils on a cold body and bid farewell to the one man who gave reason to their hopes.

But it isn't hope that leads the women up the mountain to the tomb. It is duty. Naked devotion. They expect nothing in return. What could Jesus give? What could a dead man offer? The two women are not climbing the mountain to receive; they are going to the tomb to give. Period.

There is no motivation more noble.

There are times when we, too, are called to love, expecting nothing in return. Times when we are called to give money to people who will never say thanks, to forgive those who won't forgive us, to come early and stay late when no one else notices.

Service prompted by duty. This is the call of discipleship.

1. What does 1 Peter 2:7 say Jesus is to those who believe in him?

_____

_____

2. Even though their Lord had died, the two Marys sought to serve him. How does 1 Samuel 12:24 describe this kind of love?

_____

_____

3. These two women conspired to take care of a heartbreakingly difficult task. That was the strength of their devotion to Jesus. How did they demonstrate the message of Romans 12:10–11?

_____

_____

Mary and Mary knew a task had to be done—Jesus' body had to be prepared for burial. Peter didn't offer to do it. Andrew didn't volunteer. The forgiven adulteress and healed lepers are nowhere to be seen. So the two Marys decide to do it.

I wonder if halfway to the tomb they had sat down and reconsidered. What if they'd looked at each other and shrugged? "What's the use?" What if they had given up? What if one had thrown up her arms in frustration and bemoaned, "I'm tired of being the only one who cares. Let Andrew do something for a change. Let Nathaniel show some leadership"?

Whether or not they were tempted to, I'm glad they didn't quit. That would have been tragic. You see, we know something they didn't. We know the Father was watching. Mary and Mary thought they were alone. They weren't. They thought their journey was unnoticed. They were wrong. God knew. He was watching them walk up the mountain. He was measuring their steps. He was smiling at their hearts and thrilled at their devotion. And he had a surprise waiting for them.

4. God has always rewarded faithfulness. What does Isaiah 50:10 urge?

_____

_____

5. What sight was waiting just around the corner for these two women, according to Matthew 28:2–4?

_____

_____

Now, read that passage again carefully; this is what I noticed for the first time today.

> Why did the angel move the stone? For whom did he roll away the rock?
>
> For Jesus? That's what I always thought. I just assumed that the angel moved the stone so Jesus could come out. But think about it. Did the stone have to be removed in order for Jesus to exit? Did God have to have help? Was the death conqueror so weak that he couldn't push away a rock? ("Hey, could somebody out there move this rock so I can get out?")
>
> I don't think so. The text gives the impression that Jesus was already out when the stone was moved! Nowhere do the Gospels say that the angel moved the stone for Jesus. For whom, then, was the stone moved?
>
> Listen to what the angel says: "Come and see the place where his body was" (Matthew 28:6 NCV).

The stone was moved—not for Jesus—but for the women; not so Jesus could come out, but so the women could see in!

Mary looks at Mary, and Mary is grinning the same grin she had when the bread and fish kept coming out of the basket. The old passion flares. Suddenly it's all right to dream again.

"Go quickly and tell his followers, 'Jesus has risen from the dead. He is going into Galilee ahead of you, and you will see him there'" (Matthew 28:7 NCV).

Mary and Mary don't have to be told twice. They turn and start running to Jerusalem. The darkness is gone. The sun is up. The Son is out. But the Son isn't finished.

One surprise still awaits them.

"Suddenly, Jesus met them and said, 'Greetings.' The women came up to him, took hold of his feet, and worshiped him. Then Jesus said to them, 'Don't be afraid. Go and tell my followers to go on to Galilee, and they will see me there'" (vv. 9–10 NCV).

The God of surprises strikes again. It's as if he said, "I can't wait any longer. They came this far to see me; I'm going to drop in on them."

God does that for the faithful. Just when the womb gets too old for babies, Sarai gets pregnant. Just when the failure is too great for grace, David is pardoned. And just when the road is too dark for Mary and Mary, the angel glows, and the Savior shows, and the two women will never be the same.

The lesson? Three words. Don't give up.

Is the trail dark? Don't sit.

Is the road long? Don't stop.

Is the night black? Don't quit.

6. Even when it's difficult. Even when it seems impossible. Even when we don't understand why. What does Jesus say in Mark 9:23?

_____

_____

7. What plea follows immediately after the Lord's declaration?

_____

_____

Do not be afraid;
only believe.

MARK 5:36

8. What are we invited to do in John 14:1?

_____

_____

9. The story of the two Marys is a story of devotion and diligence and delight. What hope does it give you as you consider the prayer of Hebrews 6:11?

_____

_____

God is watching. For all you know, right at this moment he may be telling the angel to move the stone.

The check may be in the mail.

The apology may be in the making.

The job contract may be on the desk.

Don't quit. For if you do, you may miss the answer to your prayers.

God still sends angels. And God still moves stones. ✳

I'VE ALWAYS PERCEIVED JOHN as a fellow who viewed life simply. "Right is right and wrong is wrong, and things aren't nearly as complicated as we make them out to be."

For example, defining Jesus would be a challenge to the best of writers, but John handles the task with casual analogy. The Messiah, in a word, was "the Word." A walking message. A love letter. Be he a fiery verb or a tender adjective, he was, quite simply, a word.

And life? Well, life is divided into two sections, light and darkness. If you are in one, you are not in the other and vice versa.

When Jesus therefore saw His mother, and the disciple whom He loved standing by, He said to His mother, "Woman, behold your son!"
JOHN 19:26

1. John spoke of Jesus as the Word in all of his writings. What does each of the following verses tell us about the Word?

   John 1:1 _____

   John 1:14 _____

   1 John 1:1_____

   Revelation 19:13_____

2. What other comparisons does John draw in John 1:1–5?

   _____

   _____

3. Jesus didn't just bring light and life. He *is* light and life!

- What does Paul call Christ in Colossians 3:4?

_____

_____

- In John 8:12, what does Jesus claim to be?

_____

_____

- What picture are we presented with in Revelation 21:23?

_____

_____

Next question?

"The devil is the father of lies, and the Messiah is the father of truth. God is love, and you are in his corner if you love, too. In fact, most problems are solved by loving one another."

And sometimes, when the theology gets a bit thick, John pauses just long enough to offer a word of explanation. Because of this patient storytelling, we have the classic commentary, "God so loved the world that he gave his one and only Son" (John 3:16 NIV).

But I like John most for the way he loved Jesus. His relationship with Jesus was, again, rather simple. To John, Jesus was a good friend with a good heart and a good idea. A once-upon-a-time storyteller with a somewhere-over-the-rainbow promise.

4. What are the familiar maxims of friendship found in Proverbs 17:17 and Proverbs 18:24?

_____

_____

5. In Matthew 9:15, Jesus defends his followers by comparing them to what? What coming event is he referring to here?

_____

_____

6. What shift in relationships does Jesus express in John 15:14–15?

_____

7. What expression of love do we find in John 15:13?

_____

_____

One gets the impression that to John, Jesus was above all a loyal companion. Messiah? Yes. Son of God? Indeed. Miracle worker? That, too. But more than anything Jesus was a pal. Someone you could go camping with or bowling with or count the stars with.

Simple. To John, Jesus wasn't a treatise on social activism, nor was he a license for blowing up abortion clinics or living in a desert. Jesus was a friend.

Now, what do you do with a friend? (Well, that's rather simple too.) You stick by him.

Maybe that is why John is the only one of the twelve who was at the cross. He came to say good-bye. By his own admission he hadn't quite put the pieces together yet. But that didn't really matter. As far as he was concerned, his closest friend was in trouble, and he came to help.

"Can you take care of my mother?"

Of course. That's what friends are for.

John teaches us that the strongest relationship with Christ may not necessarily be a complicated one. He teaches us that the greatest webs of loyalty are spun, not with airtight theologies or foolproof philosophies, but with friendships—stubborn, selfless, joyful friendships.

Peace to you.
Our friends greet you.
Greet the friends by name.
3 JOHN 1:14

After witnessing this stubborn love, we are left with a burning desire to have one like it. We are left feeling that if we could have been in anyone's sandals that day, we would have been in young John's and would have been the one to offer a smile of loyalty to this dear Lord.

Selections throughout this lesson were taken from *Six Hours One Friday, When God Whispers Your Name, Just Like Jesus, He Still Moves Stones,* and *No Wonder They Call Him Savior.*

NOTES

NOTES

LESSON SIX

He's Reassuring

A PARTY was the last thing Mary Magdalene expected as she approached the tomb on that Sunday morning. The last few days had brought nothing to celebrate. The Jews could celebrate—Jesus was out of the way. The soldiers could celebrate—their work was done. But Mary couldn't celebrate. To her the last few days had brought nothing but tragedy.

Mary had been there. She had heard the leaders clamor for Jesus' blood. She had witnessed the Roman whip rip the skin off his back. She had winced as the thorns sliced his brow and had wept at the weight of the cross.

In the Louvre there is a painting of the scene of the cross. In the painting the stars are dead and the world is wrapped in darkness. In the shadows there is a kneeling form. It is Mary. She is holding her hands and lips against the bleeding feet of the Christ.

We don't know if Mary did that, but we know she could have. She was there. She was there to hold her arm around

Jesus said to her, "Woman, why are you weeping? Whom are you seeking?" She, supposing Him to be the gardener, said to Him, "Sir, if You have carried Him away, tell me where You have laid Him, and I will take Him away."
JOHN 20:15

the shoulder of Mary the mother of Jesus. She was there to close his eyes. She was there.

So it's not surprising that she wants to be there again.

In the early morning mist she arises from her mat, takes her spices and aloes, and leaves her house, past the Gate of Gennath and up to the hillside. She anticipates a somber task. By now the body will be swollen. His face will be white. Death's odor will be pungent.

A gray sky gives way to gold as she walks up the narrow trail. As she rounds the final bend, she gasps. The rock in front of the grave is pushed back.

"Someone took the body." She runs to awaken Peter and John. They rush to see for themselves. She tries to keep up with them but can't.

Peter comes out of the tomb bewildered, and John comes out believing, but Mary just sits in front of it weeping. The two men go home and leave her alone with her grief.

But something tells her she is not alone. Maybe she hears a noise. Maybe she hears a whisper. Or maybe she just hears her own heart tell her to take a look for herself.

Whatever the reason, she does. She stoops down, sticks her head into the hewn entrance, and waits for her eyes to adjust to the dark.

"Why are you crying?" She sees what looks to be a man, but he's white—radiantly white. He is one of two lights on either end of the vacant slab. Two candles blazing on an altar.

"Why are you crying?" An uncommon question to be asked in a cemetery. In fact, the question is rude. That is, unless the questioner knows something the questionee doesn't.

"They have taken my Lord away, and I don't know where they have put him" (John 20:13 NIV).

She still calls him "my Lord." As far as she knows, his lips are silent. As far as she knows, his corpse has been carted off by grave robbers. But in spite of it all, he is still her Lord.

Such devotion moves Jesus. It moves him closer to her. So close she hears him breathing. She turns, and there he stands. She thinks he is the gardener.

Now, Jesus could have revealed himself at this point. He could have called for an angel to present him or a band to announce his presence. But he didn't.

"Why are you crying? Who is it you are looking for?" (v. 15 NIV).

He doesn't leave her wondering long, just long enough to remind us that he loves to surprise us. He waits for us to despair of human strength and then intervenes with heavenly. God waits for us to give up and then—surprise!

Has it been a while since you let God surprise you? It's easy to reach the point where we have God figured out.

1. What pleases God, according to 1 Corinthians 1:21?

_____

_____

After all, he's famous for great and unexpected acts; there's no end to his surprises.

JOB 5:9 MSG

2. In 1 Corinthians 1:27, what does Paul tell us the Lord loves to choose? Why?

_____

_____

We'll never comprehend all the great things he does; his miracle-surprises can't be counted.

JOB 9:10 MSG

3. God is fond of the unexpected. When carrying out his purposes, he often takes a route no one would have anticipated. How are these qualities described in Job 5:9 and Job 9:10?

_____

_____

God appearing at the strangest of places. Doing the strangest of things. Stretching smiles where there had hung only frowns. Placing twinkles where there were only tears. Hanging a bright star in a dark sky. Arching rainbows in the midst of thunderclouds. Calling names in a cemetery.

"Miriam," he said softly, "surprise!"

Mary was shocked. It's not often you hear your name spoken by an eternal tongue. But when she did, she recognized it. And when she did, she responded correctly. She worshiped him.

4. Jesus warned the disciples that sorrow would come. What were his words in John 16:20?

_____

_____

5. What did he compare their sorrow and pain to in John 16:21? Can you attest to the truth of his words from personal experience? If so, explain.

_____

_____

6. What is the promise at the end of John 16:22?

_____

_____

They shall obtain joy and gladness, and sorrow and sighing shall flee away.

ISAIAH 35:10

7. Mary was surprised by joy, and someday we'll know the same thrill. To what are we looking forward, according to 1 Thessalonians 2:19?

_____

_____

8. What do we have in store, according to 1 Corinthians 2:9?

_____

_____

The scene has all the elements of a surprise party—secrecy, wide eyes, amazement, gratitude. But this celebration is timid in comparison with the one that is being planned for the future. It will be similar to Mary's, but a lot bigger. Many more graves will open. Many more names will be called. Many more knees will bow. And many more seekers will celebrate.

It's going to be some party. I plan to make sure my name is on the guest list. How about you? ✳

DAY TWO
Touch and see . . .

Then He said to Thomas, "Reach your finger here, and look at My hands; and reach your hand here, and put it into My side. Do not be unbelieving, but believing."
JOHN 20:27

THOMAS. He defies tidy summary.

Oh, I know we've labeled him. Somewhere in some sermon somebody called him "Doubting Thomas." And the nickname stuck. And it's true, he *did* doubt. It's just that there was more to it than that. There was more to his questioning than a simple lack of faith. It was more due to a lack of imagination. You see it in more than just the resurrection story.

Consider, for instance, the time that Jesus was talking in all eloquence about the home he was going to prepare. Though the imagery wasn't easy for Thomas to grasp, he was doing his best. You can see his eyes filling his face as he tries to envision a big white house on St. Thomas Avenue. And just when Thomas is about to get the picture, Jesus assumes, "You know the way where I am going" (John 14:4 RSV). Thomas blinks a time or two, looks around at the other blank faces, and then bursts out with candid aplomb, "Lord, we don't know where you are going, so how can we know the way?" (John 14:5 NIV). Thomas didn't mind speaking his mind. If you don't understand something, say so! His imagination would only stretch so far.

And then there was the time that Jesus told his disciples he was going to go be with Lazarus even though Lazarus was already dead and buried. Thomas couldn't imagine what Jesus was referring to, but if Jesus was wanting to go back into the arena with those Jews who had tried once before to stone him, Thomas wasn't going to let him face them alone. So he patted his trusty sidearm and said, "Let's die with him!" Thomas had spent his life waiting on the Messiah, and now that the Messiah was here, Thomas was willing to spend his life for him. Not much imagination, but a lot of loyalty.

Perhaps it is this trait of loyalty that explains why Thomas wasn't in the Upper Room when Jesus appeared to the other apostles. You see, I think Thomas took the death of Jesus pretty hard. Even though he couldn't quite comprehend all the metaphors that Jesus at times employed, he was still willing to go to the end with him. But he had never expected that the end would come so abruptly and prematurely. As a result, Thomas was left with a crossword puzzle full of unanswered riddles.

On the one hand, the idea of a resurrected Jesus was too far-fetched for dogmatic Thomas. His limited creativity left little room for magic or razzle-dazzle. Besides, he wasn't about to set himself up to be disappointed again. One disappointment was enough, thank you. Yet, on the other hand, his loyalty made him yearn to believe. As long as there was the slimmest thread of hope, he wanted to be counted in.

His turmoil, then, came from a fusion of his lack of imagination and his unwavering loyalty. He was too honest with life to be gullible and yet was too loyal to Jesus to be unfaithful. In the end, it was this realistic devotion that caused him to utter the now famous condition: "Unless I see the nail marks in his hands and put my finger where the nails were . . . I will not believe it" (John 20:25 NIV).

So, I guess you could say that he did doubt. But it was a different kind of doubting that springs not from timidity or mistrust but from a reluctance to believe the impossible and a simple fear of being hurt twice.

Most of us are the same way, aren't we? In our world of budgets, long-range planning, and computers, don't we find it hard to trust in the unbelievable? Don't most of us tend to scrutinize life behind furrowed brows and walk with cautious steps? It's hard for us to imagine that God can surprise us. To make a little room for miracles today, well, it's not sound thinking.

As a result, we, like Thomas, find it hard to believe that God can do the very thing that he is best at: replacing death with life. Our infertile imaginations bear little hope that the improbable will occur. We then, like Thomas, let our dreams fall victim to doubt.

We make the same mistake that Thomas made: we forget that "impossible" is one of God's favorite words.

1. God's ways are often described as awesome and marvelous, wonderful and unsearchable.

   • What are we urged to remember in 1 Chronicles 28:9?

   _____

   _____

   • How does Psalm 118:23 describe that which the Lord does?

   _____

   _____

   • What is the song in Revelation 15:3? What does it say about the Lord?

   _____

   _____

2. What does God invite us to see in Isaiah 29:14? Will the wise man comprehend it or the prudent and intelligent man understand it?

   _____

   _____

3. Jesus states it plainly in Matthew 19:26. Where does he draw the line between the possible and the impossible?

_____

_____

4. With that in mind, how would you answer the question raised in Acts 26:8?

_____

_____

5. All along the way Jesus spoke of what was coming. He told his disciples things they wouldn't understand until they had the benefit of hindsight. Why did he do this, according to John 13:19 and John 14:29?

_____

_____

6. What did Jesus urge Thomas to become in John 20:27?

_____

_____

7. Thomas and company were just the beginning. Whom did Jesus pray for in John 17:20?

_____

_____

For since the beginning of the world men have not heard nor perceived by the ear, nor has the eye seen any God besides You, who acts for the one who waits for Him.

ISAIAH 64:4

Then He said to Thomas, "Reach your finger here, and look at My hands; and reach your hand here, and put it into My side. Do not be unbelieving, but believing."

JOHN 20:27

8. What blessing does Jesus declare in John 20:29?

_____

_____

9. In the face of the impossible, all we can do is believe. In the face of doubt, how do the words of Hebrews 11:1–2 reassure us?

_____

_____

How about you? How is your imagination these days? When was the last time you let some of your dreams elbow out your logic? When was the last time you imagined the unimaginable? When was the last time you dreamed of an entire world united in peace or all believers united in fellowship? When was the last time you dared dream of the day when every mouth will be fed and every nation will dwell in peace? When was the last time you dreamed about every creature on earth hearing about the Messiah? Has it been a while since you claimed God's promise to do "more than all we ask or imagine" (Ephesians 3:20 NIV)?

Though it went against every logical bone in his body, Thomas said he would believe if he could have just a little proof. And Jesus (who is ever so patient with our doubting) gave Thomas exactly what he requested. He extended his hands one more time. And was Thomas ever surprised. He did a double take, fell flat on his face, and cried, "My Lord and my God!" (John 20:28 NIV).

Jesus must have smiled.

He knew he had a winner in Thomas. Anytime you mix loyalty with a little imagination, you've got a man of God on your hands. A man who will die for a truth. Just look at Thomas. Legend has him hopping a freighter to India where they had to kill him to get him to quit talking about his home prepared in the world to come and his friend who came back from the dead. ✳

DAY THREE

Peace be
with you . . .

Then, the same day at evening, being the first day of the week, when the doors were shut where the disciples were assembled, for fear of the Jews, Jesus came and stood in the midst, and said to them, "Peace be with you."
JOHN 20:19

THE CHURCH OF JESUS CHRIST began with a group of frightened men in a second-floor room in Jerusalem.

Though trained and taught, they didn't know what to say. Though they'd marched with him for three years, they now sat . . . afraid. They were timid soldiers, reluctant warriors, speechless messengers.

Their most courageous act was to get up and lock the door.

Some looked out the window, some looked at the wall, some looked at the floor, but all looked inside themselves.

And well they should, for it was an hour of self-examination. All their efforts seemed so futile. Nagging their memories were the promises they'd made but not kept. When the Roman soldiers took Jesus, Jesus' followers took off. With the very wine of the covenant on their breath and the bread of his sacrifice in their bellies, they fled.

All those boasts of bravado? All those declarations of devotion? They lay broken and shattered at the gate of Gethsemane's garden.

1. The Lord was betrayed by one of his own. What deal did Judas broker in Matthew 26:14–16?

_____

_____

2. Jesus was denied by the very one who'd been swiftest to his defense. What were Peter's words in Matthew 26:73–74?

_____

_____

3. When faced with the multitude, what did the disciples do, according to Matthew 26:55–56?

_____

_____

We don't know where the disciples went when they fled the garden, but we do know what they took: a memory. They took a heart-stopping memory of a man who called himself no less than God in the flesh. And they couldn't get him out of their minds. Try as they might to lose him in the crowd, they couldn't forget him. If they saw a leper, they thought of his compassion. If they heard a storm, they would remember the day he silenced one. If they saw a child, they would think of the day he held one. And if they saw a lamb being carried to the temple, they would remember his face streaked with blood and his eyes flooded with love.

No, they couldn't forget him. As a result, they came back. And, as a result, the church of our Lord began with a group of frightened men in an upper room.

Just as someone mumbles, "It's no use," they hear a noise. They hear a voice.

"Peace be with you" (John 20:19 NIV).

4. What is God's relationship to peace, according to 1 Corinthians 14:33?

_____

_____

5. The disciples sorely needed peace, and the God of peace—Peace itself—walked through the door. Match up the following passages with their messages about peace.

___ Isaiah 26:12   a. Live in peace.

___ Romans 5:1   b. Pursue the things that make for peace.

___ Romans 14:19   c. The Lord establishes peace.

___ Romans 15:33   d. God is the God of peace.

___ 2 Corinthians 13:11   e. Christ is our peace.

___ Ephesians 2:13–14   f. We have peace with God through Jesus.

___ Colossians 1:20   g. Peace was made through the blood of his cross.

6. What assurance can we receive from the words of Christ in John 16:33?

_____

_____

7. In John 14:27 we have a similar promise. What does Jesus leave to us?

_____

_____

Every head lifted. Every eye turned. Every mouth dropped open. Someone looked at the door.

It was still locked.

It was a moment the apostles would never forget, a story they would never cease to tell. The stone of the tomb was not enough to keep him *in*. The walls of the room were not enough to keep him *out*.

The one betrayed sought his betrayers. What did he say to them? Not "What a bunch of flops!" Not "I told you so." No "Where-were-you-when-I-needed-you?" speeches. But simply one phrase: "Peace be with you." The very thing they didn't have was the very thing he offered: peace.

It was too good to be true! So amazing was the appearance that some were saying, "Pinch me; I'm dreaming" even at the ascension. No wonder they returned to Jerusalem with great joy! No wonder they were always in the temple praising God!

A transformed group stood beside a transformed Peter as he announced some weeks later: "Therefore let all Israel be assured of this: God has made this Jesus, whom you crucified, both Lord and Christ" (Acts 2:36 NIV).

No timidity in his words. No reluctance. About three thousand people believed his message.

The apostles sparked a movement. The people became followers of the death-conqueror. They couldn't hear enough or say enough about him. People began to call them "Christians." Christ was their model, their message. They preached "Jesus Christ and him crucified," not for the lack of another topic, but because they couldn't exhaust this one (1 Corinthians 2:2 NIV).

What unlocked the doors of the apostles' hearts?

Simple. They saw Jesus. They encountered the Christ. Their sins collided with their Savior, and their Savior won! What lit the boiler of the apostles was a red-hot conviction that the very one who should have sent them to hell went to hell for them and came back to tell about it. ✳

The sun was in the water before Peter noticed it—a wavy circle of gold on the surface of the sea. A fisherman is usually the first to spot the sun rising over the crest of the hills. It means his night of labor is finally over.

But when the morning had now come, Jesus stood on the shore; yet the disciples did not know that it was Jesus.
JOHN 21:4

But not for this fisherman. Though the light reflected on the lake, the darkness lingered in Peter's heart. The wind chilled, but he didn't feel it. His friends slept soundly, but he didn't care. The nets at his feet were empty, the sea had been a miser, but Peter wasn't thinking about that.

His thoughts were far from the Sea of Galilee. His mind was in Jerusalem, reliving an anguished night. As the boat rocked, his memories raced:

the clanking of the Roman guard,

the flash of a sword and the duck of a head,

a touch for Malchus, a rebuke for Peter,

soldiers leading Jesus away.

"What was I thinking?" Peter mumbled to himself as he stared at the bottom of the boat. *Why did I run?*

Peter had run; he had turned his back on his dearest friend and run. We don't know where. Peter may not have known where. He found a hole, a hut, an abandoned shed— he found a place to hide, and he hid.

He had bragged, "Everyone else may stumble . . . but I will not" (Matthew 26:33 NCV). Yet he did. Peter did what he swore he wouldn't do. He had tumbled face first into the pit of his own fears. And there he sat. All he could hear was his hollow promise. *Everyone else may stumble . . . but I will not. Everyone else . . . I will not. I will not. I will not.* A war raged within the fisherman.

At that moment the instinct to survive collided with his allegiance to Christ, and for just a moment allegiance won. Peter stood and stepped out of hiding and followed the noise till he saw the torch-lit jury in the courtyard of Caiaphas.

He stopped near a fire and warmed his hands. The fire sparked with irony. The night had been cold. The fire was hot. But Peter was neither. He was lukewarm.

"Peter followed at a distance," Luke described (Luke 22:54 NIV).

He was loyal . . . from a distance.

This wasn't the first night that Peter had spent on the Sea of Galilee. After all, he was a fisherman. He, like the others, worked at night. He knew the fish would feed near the surface during the cool of the night and return to the deep during the day. No, this wasn't the first night Peter had spent on the Sea of Galilee. Nor was it the first night he had caught nothing.

There was that time years before . . .

Most mornings Peter and his partners would sell their fish, repair their nets, and head home to rest with a bag of money and a feeling of satisfaction. This particular morning there was no money. There was no satisfaction. They had worked all through the night but had nothing to show for it except weary backs and worn nets.

And, what's worse, everyone knew it. Every morning the shore would become a market as the villagers came to buy their fish, but that day there were no fish.

Jesus was there that morning, teaching. As the people pressed, there was little room for him to stand, so he asked Peter if his boat could be a platform. Peter agreed, maybe thinking the boat might as well be put to some good use.

Peter listens as Jesus teaches. It's good to hear something other than the slapping of waves. When Jesus finishes with the crowd, he turns to Peter. He has another request. He wants to go fishing. "Take the boat into deep water, and put your nets in the water to catch some fish" (Luke 5:4 NCV).

Please understand that the main character in this drama of denial is not Peter, but Jesus. Jesus, who knows the hearts of all people, knew the denial of his friend. Three times the salt of Peter's betrayal stung the wounds of the Messiah.

HE STILL MOVES STONES

Peter groans. The last thing he wants to do is fish. The boat is clean. The nets are ready to dry. The sun is up and he is tired. It's time to go home. Besides, everyone is watching. They've already seen him come back empty-handed once. And, what's more, what does Jesus know about fishing?

So Peter speaks. "Master, we worked hard all night trying to catch fish" (v. 5 NCV).

Mark the weariness in the words.

"We worked hard." Scraping the hull. Carrying the nets. Pulling the oars. Throwing the nets high into the moonlit sky. Listening as they slapped on the surface of the water.

"All night." The sky had gone from burnt orange to midnight black to morning gold. The hours had passed as slowly as the fleets of clouds before the moon. The fishermen's conversation had stilled, and their shoulders ached. While the village slept, the men worked. All . . . night . . . long.

"Trying to catch fish." The night's events had been rhythmic: net swung and tossed high till it spread itself against the sky. Then wait. Let it sink. Pull it in. Do it again. Throw. Pull. Throw. Pull. Throw. Pull. Every toss had been a prayer. But every drag of the empty net had come back unanswered. Even the net sighed as the men pulled it out and prepared to throw it again.

For twelve hours they'd fished. And now . . . now Jesus is wanting to fish some more? And not just off the shore but in the deep?

Peter sees his friends shrug their shoulders. He looks at the people on the beach watching him. He doesn't know what to do. Jesus may know a lot about a lot, but Peter knows about fishing. Peter knows when to work and when to quit. He knows there is a time to go on and a time to get out.

Common sense said it was time to get out. Logic said cut your losses and go home. Experience said pack it up and get some rest. But Jesus said, *"We can try again if you want."*

The most difficult journey is back to the place where you failed.

Jesus knows that. That's why he volunteers to go along. "The first outing was solo; this time I'll be with you. Try it again, this time with me on board."

1. We make mistakes. We fall short. We fail. What insight does Proverbs 24:16 offer about those times when we fall?

_____

_____

2. Describe a time you tried to do something on your own—and failed.

_____

_____

_____

_____

Peter reluctantly agrees to try again. "But you say to put the nets in the water, so I will" (Luke 5:5 NCV). It didn't make any sense, but he'd been around this Nazarene enough to know that his presence made a difference. That wedding in Cana? That sick child of the royal ruler? It's as if Jesus carried his own deck to the table.

So the oars dip again, and the boat goes out. The anchor is set, and the nets fly once more.

Peter watches as the net sinks, and he waits. He waits until the net spreads as far as his rope allows. The fishermen are quiet. Peter is quiet. Jesus is quiet. Suddenly the rope yanks. The net, heavy with fish, almost pulls Peter overboard.

"John, James!" he yells. "Come quick!"

Soon the boats are so full of fish that the port side rim dips close to the surface. Peter, ankle deep in flopping silver, turns to look at Jesus, only to find that Jesus is looking at him.

That's when he realizes who Jesus is.

What an odd place to meet God—on a fishing boat on a small sea in a remote country! But such is the practice of the God who comes into our world. Such is the encounter experienced by those who are willing to try again . . . with him.

Peter's life was never again the same after that catch.

3. When we see Jesus—hear his words, trust his voice—we're changed. Does it happen all at once? Usually not. How does Paul describe the working of the Lord in our hearts in 2 Corinthians 3:18?

_____

_____

4. What is the promise of Philippians 1:6?

_____

_____

_____

He had turned his back on the sea to follow the Messiah. He had left the boats, thinking he'd never return. But now he's back. Full circle. Same sea. Same boat. Maybe even the same spot.

But this isn't the same Peter. Three years of living with the Messiah have changed him. He's seen too much. Too many walking crippled, vacated graves, too many hours hearing his words. He's not the same Peter. It's the same Galilee, but a different fisherman.

Why did he return? What brought him back to Galilee after the crucifixion? Despair? Some think so—I don't. Hope dies hard for a man who has known Jesus. I think that's what Peter has. That's what brought him back. Hope. A bizarre hope that on the sea where he knew him first, he would know him again.

So Peter is in the boat, on the lake. Once again he's fished all night. Once again the sea has surrendered nothing.

His thoughts are interrupted by a shout from the shore. "Catch any fish?" Peter and John look up. Probably a villager. "No!" they yell. "Try the other side!" the voice yells back. John looks at Peter. What harm? So out sails the net. Peter wraps the rope around his wrist to wait.

But there is no wait. The rope pulls taut, and the net catches. Peter sets his weight against the side of the boat and begins to bring in the net, reaching down, pulling up, reaching down, pulling up. He's so intense with the task, he misses the message.

John doesn't. The moment is déjà vu. This has happened before. The long night. The empty net. The call to cast again. Fish flapping on the floor of the boat. Wait a minute. He lifts his eyes to the man on the shore. "It's him," he whispers.

Then louder, "It's Jesus."

Then shouting, "It's the Lord, Peter. It's the Lord!"

Peter turns and looks. Jesus has come. Not just Jesus the teacher, but Jesus the death-defeater, Jesus the king . . . Jesus the victor over darkness. Jesus the God of heaven and earth is on the shore . . . and he's building a fire.

Peter plunges into the water, swims to the shore, and stumbles out wet and shivering and stands in front of the friend he betrayed. Jesus has prepared a bed of coals. Both are aware of the last time Peter had stood near a fire. Peter had failed God, but God had come to him.

For one of the few times in his life, Peter is silent. What words would suffice? The moment is too holy for words. God is offering breakfast to the friend who betrayed him. And Peter is once again finding grace at Galilee.

What do you say at a moment like this?

What do *you* say at a moment such as this?

It's just you and God. You and God both know what you did. And neither one of you is proud of it. What do you do?

You might consider doing what Peter did. Stand in God's presence. Stand in his sight. Stand still and wait. Sometimes that's all a soul can do. Too repentant to speak, but too hopeful to leave—we just stand.

Stand amazed.

He has come back.

He invites you to try again. This time, with him.

5. Read John 21. How does this scene end?

_____

_____

6. Many Bible characters passed through faith-altering experiences. Examine two men or women who were reminded by God of his love for them. What does the end of their stories say about similar rough patches in our lives?

_____

_____

_____

_____

_____

_____

_____

DAY FIVE
Well done . . .

His lord said to him, "Well done, good and faithful servant; you have been faithful over a few things, I will make you ruler over many things. Enter into the joy of your lord."
MATTHEW 25:23

ON ONE OF MY SHELVES is a book on power abs. The cover shows a closeup of a fellow flexing his flat belly. His gut has more ripples and ridges than a pond on a windy day. Inspired, I bought the book, read the routine, and did the sit-ups . . . for a week.

Not far from the power-abs book is a tape series on speed reading. This purchase was Denalyn's idea, but when I read the ad, I was equally enthused. The course promises to do for my mind what *Power Abs* promised to do for my gut—turn it into steel. The back-cover copy promises that mastering this six-week series will enable you to read twice as fast and retain twice the amount. All you have to do is listen to the tapes—which I intend to do . . . someday.

And then there is my bottle of essential minerals. Thirty-two ounces of pure health. One swallow a day and I'll ingest my quota of calcium, chloride, magnesium, sodium, and sixty-six other vital earthly elements. (There's even a trace of iron, which is good since I missed my shot at the iron abs and the steel-trap mind.) The enthusiast who sold me the minerals convinced me that thirty dollars was a small price to pay for good health. I agree. I just keep forgetting to take them.

Don't get me wrong. Not everything in my life is incomplete. But I confess, I don't always finish what I start. Chances are I'm not alone. Any unfinished projects under your roof? Perhaps an exercise machine whose primary function thus far has been to hold towels? Or an unopened do-it-yourself pottery course? How about a half-finished patio deck or a half-dug pool or a half-planted garden? And let's not even touch the topic of diets and weight loss, OK?

You know as well as I, it's one thing to start something. It's something else entirely to complete it. You may think I'm going to talk to you about the importance of finishing everything. Could be you are bracing yourself for a bit of chastising.

If so, relax. "Don't start what you can't finish" is not one of my points. And I'm not going to say anything about what is used to pave the road to hell. To be honest, I don't believe you should finish everything you start. (Every student with homework just perked up.) There are certain quests better left undone, some projects wisely abandoned. (Though I wouldn't list homework as one of those.)

We can become so obsessed with completion that we become blind to effectiveness. Just because a project is on the table doesn't mean it can't be returned to the shelf. No, my desire is not to convince you to finish everything. My desire is to encourage you to finish the *right* thing. Certain races are optional—like washboard abs and speed reading. Other races are essential—like the race of faith.

1. Paul pressed on toward a goal throughout his ministry.

   • What did he want to attain, according to Philippians 3:10–12?

   _____

   _____

   _____

   • What was his "secret" in running, according to verse 13?

   _____

   _____

   • According to Philippians 3:14, what was the prize?

   _____

   _____

2. Had Paul's perspective changed as he neared the end of his course? What does he say about the race of faith in 2 Timothy 4:7?

   _____

   _____

3. Reread Hebrews 12:1–2, and answer the following:

   • How should we run?

   _____

   _____

   • What should we get rid of first?

   _____

   _____

- Who's watching us?

  _____

  _____

- Where should our eyes be fixed?

  _____

  _____

- Whose example do we follow?

  _____

  _____

But those who wait on the LORD shall renew their strength; they shall mount up with wings like eagles, they shall run and not be weary, they shall walk and not faint.

ISAIAH 40:31

Had golf existed in the New Testament era, I'm sure the writers would have spoken of mulligans and foot wedges, but it didn't, so they wrote about running. The word *race* is from the Greek *agon,* from which we get the word *agony.* The Christian's race is not a jog but rather a demanding and grueling, sometimes agonizing race. It takes a massive effort to finish strong.

Likely you've noticed that many don't. Surely you've observed there are many on the side of the trail? They used to be running. There was a time when they kept the pace. But then weariness set in. They didn't think the run would be this tough. Or they were discouraged by a bump and daunted by a fellow runner. Whatever the reason, they don't run anymore. They may be Christians. They may come to church. They may put a buck in the plate and warm a pew, but their hearts aren't in the race. They retired before their time. Unless something changes, their best work will have been their first work, and they will finish with a whimper.

By contrast, Jesus' best work was his final work, and his strongest step was his last step. Our Master is the classic example of one who endured. The writer of Hebrews goes on to say that Jesus "held on while wicked people were doing evil things to him" (12:3 NCV). The Bible says Jesus "held on," implying that Jesus could have "let go." The runner could have given up, sat down, gone home. He could have quit the race. But he didn't. "He held on while wicked people were doing evil things to him."

4. What was Paul determined to do, according to Acts 20:24?

_____

_____

5. We can't give up. We must press on. John has a word he likes to use for folks who show that kind of tenacity—overcomers.

- Whom can we overcome, according to 1 John 5:5?

_____

_____

- What is the secret to our victory when we overcome, according to 1 John 5:4?

_____

_____

- Even more so, why are we able to overcome, according to 1 John 4:4?

_____

_____

I invite you to think carefully about the supreme test Jesus faced in the race. Hebrews 12:2 offers this intriguing statement: "[Jesus] accepted the shame as if it were nothing" (NCV).

Such words stir one urgent question: How? How did he endure such disgrace? What gave Jesus the strength to endure the shame of all the world? We need an answer, don't we? Like Jesus we are tempted. Like Jesus we are accused. Like Jesus we are ashamed. But unlike Jesus, we give up. We give out. We sit down. How can we keep running as Jesus did? How can our hearts have the endurance Jesus had?

By focusing where Jesus focused.

6. Where did Jesus keep his eyes, according to Hebrews 12:2?

_____

_____

Hebrews 12:2 may very well be the greatest testimony ever written about the glory of heaven. Nothing is said about golden streets or angels' wings. No reference is made to music or feasts. Even the word *heaven* is missing from the verse. But though the word is missing, the power is not.

Remember, heaven was not foreign to Jesus. He is the only person to live on earth *after* he had lived in heaven. As believers, you and I will live in heaven after time on earth, but Jesus did just the opposite. He knew heaven before he came to earth. He knew what awaited him upon his return. And knowing what awaited him in heaven enabled him to bear the shame on earth. In his final moments, Jesus focused on the joy God put before him.

7. We can be finishers. What does Paul promise will come to pass one day, according to Philippians 1:6?

_____

_____

8. Paul tells us that "not he who commends himself is approved, but whom the Lord commends" (2 Corinthians 10:18). We long to hear the words in Matthew 25:23. What are they?

_____

_____

9. What blessing shall serve as our benediction, as found in James 1:12?

_____

_____

Such a moment awaits us. In a world oblivious to power abs and speed reading, we'll take our place at the table. In an hour that has no end, we will rest. Surrounded by saints and engulfed by Jesus himself, the work will, indeed, be finished. The final harvest will have been gathered, we will be seated, and Christ will christen the meal with these words: "Well done, good and faithful servant."

And in that moment, the race will have been worth it.

Selections throughout this lesson are taken from *Six Hours One Friday, No Wonder They Call Him the Savior, He Still Moves Stones,* and *Just Like Jesus.*

NOTES

NOTES

NOTES

Mary

Peter

Matthew

Joseph

Nicodemus

Abigail

David

Esther

Job

The Samaritan Woman

John

Rich Young Man

These classic Bible character stories are a great invitation into the heartland of God's Word.

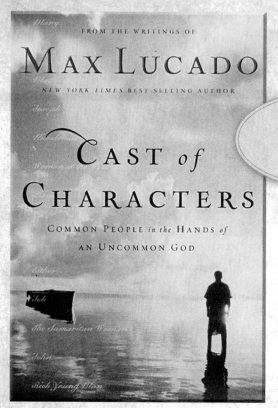

FROM THE WRITINGS OF

MAX LUCADO

NEW YORK TIMES BEST-SELLING AUTHOR

CAST of CHARACTERS

COMMON PEOPLE in the HANDS of AN UNCOMMON GOD

Available Now

Some of the most powerful stories from the Bible will come alive for today's readers through these inspiring selections from the writings of Max Lucado. Max provides a compelling look at the most high-impact moments in the biblical narrative, drawn from his previous 20+ years of writing.

At the end of each chapter will be study guide questions so the reader can go deeper.

Extraordinary stories are told about the following characters:

Mary, Peter, Matthew, Joseph, Nicodemus, Abigail, David, Esther, Job, The Samaritan Woman, John, Rich Young Man.

And more . . .